Praise for *The Older You Get the Shorter Your Stories Should Be*

"Bob Bowie's reflections on his well-lived and adventurous life are charming, funny, poignant and wise. This book is a real pleasure to read."

— Drew Faust
President Emerita, Harvard University

"Bob Bowie has written a riveting and rollicking collection of tales comprising his life as a Renaissance Man who overcame serious childhood learning disabilities to become a Harvard Poet Laureate, adventurer, lawyer and playwright. Writing with brutal candor and self-deprecating wit, Bowie unspools stories that both entertain and pack plenty of wisdom. I thoroughly enjoyed this book."

— Ben Bradlee, Jr.
*Pulitzer Prize-winning Editor of
The Boston Globe Spotlight Team*

"Pearl after pearl — brief easily accessible stories that reflect the unclouded eye of the author for all things honest, compassionate and revelatory. I laughed, cried, reflected, regretted and rejoiced reading this seemingly random collection before recognizing the common thread — clear eyed humanity. Mr. Bowie's curation of his self deprecating, poignant and often hilarious moments, will become a dear friend whose warmth and comfort are there to visit again and again!"

— Ty Cobb
*Prominent Washington, D.C. lawyer
and former White House Special Counsel*

Praise for *The Older You Get the Shorter Your Stories Should Be*

"A light, airy, and casual journey of thought-provoking reminiscence, surprisingly full of wisdom, leaving the reader with a cumulative impression of hope, innocence and possibility!"

— Stephen Eich
Producer, Former Managing Director, Steppenwolf Theater Company

"*The Older You Get* is as frank and self-effacing as its title. A life long story-teller, Bowie tells survival stories from adolescence to old age that mix the rough with the smooth— sometimes hilarious, and always bracingly honest."

— Belinda Rathbone
Biographer, historian, and fine arts journalist

"These tiny stories are a total delight. The characters and situations are filled with empathy, affection and humor. This is a truly wonderful read."

— Katya Chelli
Documentary filmmaker

"What a life Bob has had! Amusing and thought-provoking... Take five minutes to dip into Bob Bowie, or get comfortable and while away several hours. You'll be glad you did!"

— Mel Edden
Poet

The Older You Get the Shorter Your Stories Should Be

The Older You Get the Shorter Your Stories Should Be

Robert R. Bowie, Jr.

RobertBowieJr.com
facebook.com/robertbowiejrplaywright
twitter.com/robertbowiejr
instagram.com/robertbowiejr

www.saltwatermedia.com

Copyright © 2024 by Robert R. Bowie, Jr.
All rights reserved.

First Edition

ISBN 978-1-62806-422-3 (hardcover)
ISBN 978-1-62806-420-9 (softcover)
ISBN 978-1-62806-423-0 (ebook)
LCCN 2024917236

Published by Salt Water Media
29 Broad Street, Suite 104
Berlin, MD 21811
www.saltwatermedia.com

Printed in the USA.

Photos from Flickr are credited to the copyright holder and licensed under Creative Commons: creativecommons.org/licenses/by/2.0/, creativecommons.org/licenses/by-sa/2.0/, creativecommons.org/licenses/by-nd/2.0/

All characters and other entities appearing in this work are fictitious. Any resemblance to real persons, dead or alive, or other real-life entities, past or present, is purely coincidental.

Designed by Parker Bennett.

No part of this book may be used or reproduced in any matter whatsoever without written permission from the author, except in the case of brief quotations in critical articles and reviews.

Author website: www.RobertBowieJr.com

To Susan, and our families past and present,
and to our friends who carry us with them.

Contents

Preface xi

Traveling Man
You Think You've Been Embarrassed? 5
Forever Young 11
My Effort to Avoid Thinking About American Politics 17
Learning to Live Rather than Litigate 23

Friends & Family
Dancing School 29
Our Culture as the Hands of a Sculptor 33
More and More These Days I Find Myself
Waiting for the Answering Machine 39
Once Upon a Time I Had the Darwin Award
Snatched from My Grasp 43
About Dizlxia 49
Calling the Chickens Home 53
Just Out of Reach 57
Learning to Accept Love 63

People & Politics
An Offer and Acceptance 69
I Almost Got a Chance to Cite the Constitution in Traffic Court 73
It Is Different Now, but It Remains the Same 77
The Rebirth of the Heroes 83

Poets & Professors
Yes, Love Grows Forever 89
A Little Pat on the Back from a Long Time Ago 95
Elizabeth Bishop, Cemeteries, and Contrast as Creativity 101
Life after Nitrogen Narcosis? 105
Chum in the Water 109

Contents

Townie in Cambridge

From Before the Beginning 115
A Halloween Ghost Story. 119
How the Hell Did You Get into They'a?. 123
There Is Something Wonderful About Random Spontaneity! 129
Don't Settle for a Low Paying Job. Be a Poet Laureate! 133
A Walk-Off Ninth-Inning Home Run 139

It Can't Happen Here

"It Can't Happen Here". 147
Long Ago: A Tale of Two Sonnets 151
Redemption and a Big Divot in World History 155
Back to the Future 159
The World We Choose to Make 163

Courage

"The Believers" and "The Nonbelievers" 169
Fear Separates Heroes from Cowards 173
How the Definition of Courage Changes 179
In Search of a Lost Friend 185
Let's Get This Party Started 191
My Heart Is Broken but I Saw Love 195

The Practice of Law

Taking Flight 201
Red Light Green Light 207
A Trying Trial 211
The Creation and History of the Stuffed Shirt Award 217
Trial Strategy Learned from a Chicken 221
Sometimes the Best Judge or Jury is Laughter 227

Contents

Does Anybody Really Know What Time It Is?

The Question I Was Afraid to Answer 233
Does Anybody Really Know What Time It Is? 237
The Christmas I Realized 243

Writing for the Theater

Why Did I Ever Write for Theater? 249
Teaching Law Through Playwriting 255
The View from the Back 259
Sometimes the Unthinkable Just Happens 263
Sometimes You Have to Open the
Windows and Listen to the Rain 267

A Place to Be

Have You Ever Seen "The Sandlot"? 273
A Miracle in Rhinestones 275
A Way of Knowing 283
Out of the Rain and into Ice House Pond 287

Acknowkedgments 290
About the Author 293

Preface

Each year on my birthday, an involuntary jingle pops into my head:

*"Happy birthday! Happy birthday! Happy birthday to me.
The older you get the shorter your stories should be"*

I recognized it as probably good advice that didn't apply to me because I wasn't entirely committed to following this instruction.

I sought additional advice.

When I asked one of my contemporaries if he also tended to love telling interesting stories, he looked at me and responded, "Yes, I do, but my children tell me, just as I'm getting to the interesting part:

"'Land the plane, Dad!'"

I looked back on my work life and remembered that, not only was I accused of telling stories that were slightly on the longish side, I was also accused of being a repeater.

Several years ago, in the lunchroom, I agreed that if anybody could finish my story, I would stop telling it.

My introduction, which could have been a tiny bit longer, will, in fact, be evidence of my new commitment to brevity.

Here goes:

After I retired, I decided to start a second career as a poet and writer for professional theater. This is something I had always wanted to do but I was woefully unprepared.

I decided to start at the top.

I applied to Yale School of Drama, and my pitch offered Yale the great opportunity of accepting the oldest person ever to have applied. I now have the distinction of being the oldest person ever rejected.

I didn't give up.

I decided to take classes at the Commercial Theater Institute in New York City because the biggest problem I was going to have was getting anybody to read an old man script, but I had a Plan B.

I took a class in "producing." Then, during lunch breaks, when each person in the class talked about what they wanted to produce, when it was my turn I said "I don't want to produce anything. I want you to produce me."

It worked. A producer who liked one of my plays advised me to create a humorous blog with the theme "living life in the arts as a second career."

I was referred to Parker Bennett of Aligned Online and Katie Marinello of KTCommunications, who are masters of online communications.

Off I went into the unknown.

The first thing I learned was that I was too old to be of interest to agents, and the second was I knew no one in the theater or publishing world.

From the beginning, each week on Tuesdays, Parker and I would meet on Zoom to review and edit a blog that I had just finished. It would be posted on Facebook at 3:00 p.m. and immediately thereafter on my website, *robertbowiejr.com*. Then it would be forwarded to Katie who would post it on Instagram, LinkedIn, and what used to be Twitter.

Each week I posted little vignettes about all the wonderful people I met in the theater world, and how I traveled to Los Angeles, San Francisco and New York for staged readings and networking. It was a new world, and it was wonderful to discover and write about it.

Life was good. We were accomplishing the impossible. I was religious in my weekly output, and we gathered an unlikely following.

Then came March of 2020. Covid shut down the New York theaters and I had nothing to write about on my theme, so I went astray.

It was a very interesting time. I drifted into political commentary, social observations and, eventually, into people I had met and known. Remarkably, I did not lose the following for the blog, but it went pretty far afield the longer the theaters were closed.

As time went by, Parker and Katie suggested that we take the best of the blogs, eliminate most of the political and social commentary, and revisit the personal stories about people and places, things and humor.

This book is composed of what I hope are the best of these two- to three-page stories. They are not organized chronologically. They touch on a theme, find a thread and move on.

I hope they make you laugh, find joy and, perhaps occasionally, even shed a tear. Many are personal and harvested from memory because there wasn't much going on outside except Covid and politics.

Thank you. I will now land the plane.

The Older You Get the
Shorter Your Stories Should Be

Traveling Man

The Older You Get the Shorter Your Stories Should Be

You Think You've Been Embarrassed?

You think you've been embarrassed? Well, I've got you beat.

First, it all happened to me on the other side of the planet so I couldn't go home, turn off the lights and put my head under the pillow.

It happened in Xi'an, China, in an airport the morning I was scheduled to fly to Chongqing to see a panda sanctuary, then board a boat to go down the Yangtze river through the Three Gorges, and then down to Shanghai.

Second, I was traveling with a small group and the Xi'an Airport was huge, so I had nowhere to hide as my embarrassment went on and on and on…

It all started innocently at dinner the night before we were scheduled to fly out of the Xi'an airport the next morning. Our guide addressed the group and informed us that because our plane left so early the next day we all must have our bags packed and outside of our door by 4:30 so they could be picked up and taken to the airport before we went to breakfast.

Everything had to be packed except the clothes we would be wearing the next day and whatever toiletries we required for that morning.

We were told that those toiletries, once used, had to be carried on our person until we landed at Chongqing airport several hours later at which time we could return them to our suitcases.

After dinner that night, we all went up to our rooms, picked out the essential toiletries, which in my case was toothpaste, toothbrush, shampoo, razor, soap, and hairbrush. I also chose my clothes for the next day, which in my case, were one of my endless pairs of khaki pants, a blue long sleeve business shirt, underwear, socks and shoes.

All the rest was packed in the suitcase, which I put outside the door right before I set the alarm and went to bed.

The next morning when my alarm went off, before I showered and shaved, I peeked out the door. My suitcase was gone and on its way to the airport. I looked at the clock and measured the short time I had to get to breakfast.

After my shower, I bundled up my toiletries, put on my blue business shirt and started to pull up my khaki pants, but couldn't understand why I couldn't get them on until I realized that the only pair of pants I had to wear were actually those I had mistakenly packed, which unfortunately belonged to my teenage son.

My son has a 32-inch waist. I do not.

I was running out of time. I had to get to breakfast.

I grabbed both sides of the pants so that my fingers gripped the pockets and I hoisted as hard as I could. No progress.

Next, I lay on my back on the bed with my feet extended in the air and bounced on the bed to get maximum leverage, kicked my feet into the air and yanked with all my strength. No progress.

The top of the pants made it to maybe slightly above my crotch. I'm pretty certain I did not get the pants high enough to halfway cover my back end. Nothing.

Next, I tried straddling a chair and forcefully rode my pants like a cowboy rides a horse in order to force the crotch into submission.

I then tried jumping up and down to get maximum thrust, lift and torque. Nothing. This was not good!

I had to get to breakfast but I couldn't leave the room. This was not good at all!

I reassessed my situation.

I still had to put on my shoes and socks. I would have to roll up the bottom of the pants so that I wouldn't trip over them.

I was able to walk, but only if I could hold the top of my pants up as high as possible and walk with my knees banging together every time I took a step.

I searched the room for any possible help. I was fortunate to find yesterday's Chinese newspaper — bright with color — to cover my crotch.

It was a very long and slow elevator ride for every inch of the descent down maybe three floors, I noticed that the Chinese people in Xi'an, at least in this elevator on this particular morning, tended to be very quiet as they tried to find someplace else to look other than at my crotch.

My group at breakfast was less forgiving. They had to stop eating because they couldn't stop laughing.

Our guide tried to be helpful and encouraged me to wander the airport to find a clothing store, apparently in the hope that I could learn Mandarin instantly and acquire a pair of pants that was twice the size that any self-respecting member of the culture would never wear.

The guide was just trying to be helpful I know, but didn't seem to understand that I was really, at this point, no longer interested in clothing. I was no longer hoping to fit into the culture.

I was hoping to vanish from the face of the earth.

Everyone in the airport seemed to be walking by and rubbernecking in order to catch sight of whatever everyone else was laughing at.

I was completely hunched over, gripping my newspaper and pants, with my pant legs rolled up above my ankles and, just to add to my unlikely assimilation into the culture, I was wearing my disposable razor, shaving cream, toothbrush, toothpaste and hairbrush bundled up into a boutonniere blooming from my shirt pocket to add to my look.

The Chinese newspaper was fast becoming my most valuable asset since, as it turned out, my seat on the plane was between two meticulously dressed, very frightened Chinese businessmen who apparently feared any eye contact with me, their fellow traveler, for fear that it might prompt me to flash them.

In times like this I try to focus on making my situation into a positive learning experience.

After thinking about my situation for a little while, I concluded there wasn't a lot to learn so, in the alternative, I thought it might be helpful to try to imagine what could be worse than what was happening to me at this exact moment.

I no longer wonder what it must feel like to wear a miniskirt if you are knock kneed, but that wasn't bad enough, so I tried to imagine what it was like to wear a miniskirt, knock kneed with high heels.

I made sure that I would be the last person to leave the plane when we landed. in order to give the baggage handlers extra time so when I went to pick up my bag it would be there.

I hid in the airport men's room for a while. I was afraid I had permanently injured my lower intestines. I was sure I had bruising. I couldn't really lift or lower my pants now.

Eventually, I built up all my courage and raced through the teeming airport hunched over, with one hand holding the top of my pants and the other gripping my newspaper.

I swooped down on my bag and hauled it into the men's room, found a stall, opened the suitcase, liberated myself of my son's pants, and instantly threw them away for no good reason other than I needed to purge them.

A few months ago, I went on a trip with some of that same group that had gone on the China trip. When my story came up, I refused to relive the experience, so they went right ahead and told it anyway. They kept on embellishing the story at my expense.

The trip to China was 10 years ago, and the listeners could not stop laughing. Apparently, it gets better and better.

One person, who I am not sure was even on the China trip, claimed to have seen it all from the back and referred to it as "the morning the moon rose over the Yangtze!"

I must now live in infamy forever.

Forever Young

It is funny how a stranger's aging face will never reveal the face of its youth. However…

A little less than a month ago, I went to a beautiful warm sun-drenched October wedding on the edge of a calm harbor in New Bedford, Massachusetts.

On the lawn, an hour or so before the wedding began, a small group of old men slowly gathered and greeted each other. Some had not seen each other for almost 50 years.

We had become friends long ago during high school, as a diaspora loosely formed by outcasts of various New England schools. We had all been transferred or expelled from someplace, in several cases more than once, because of undiagnosed learning issues and/or an intransigent attitude, and thus had been prematurely released upon the world to get our education on our own terms with far less supervision.

No harm done. Most of us survived and had lived interesting lives of our own making and all of us had stories of our adventures along the way as we talked out on the lawn during that evening, or later on the phone. Nonetheless, we had bonded quite profoundly from our common experiences back then, and these stories and adventures defined who we believed we were.

As we told the stories about each other, the mask of old age dropped from our faces.

There was one friend who was not present as we rekindled old friendships and plowed through our memories.

The bride's father had included in the program an "In Memorium" section that included those who had been lost along the way. One of our lost friends, let's call him Brad, had been the bride's godfather before his death.

Brad had been lost at sea years ago.

I didn't know him as well as some of the others, but I remembered early one spring day going down to the boatyard he used on Cape Cod, and watching him paint the waterline high on his boat to cover the approximately 2 1/2 tons of contraband that he expected to be bringing back from Jamaica a little later that year.

It was his custom to avoid returning by the Windward passage where he might be apprehended and instead sail far out into the Atlantic, then head north for an extended run, and then hug the shore as he traveled south back along the coastline in order to appear to be a tourist sailing down to the Cape from Maine.

He was a brilliant unflappable sailor.

One of his friends remembered how he had sailed back with him from Morocco, along with contraband, when Brad's 37-foot-deep keeled boat suffered debilitating electrical equipment failure. Brad then navigated without the aid of instruments, solely with a sextant, and expertly traveled down to the edge of the equator. As the sun came up one morning along the expansive horizon, he had watched "a thousand little squalls, each with rainbows beneath them in the sunrise" as Brad had navigated cross the Atlantic and hit his target, Antigua, perfectly.

Once freed from formal education, Brad was largely self-schooled, but was well read in history, loved the Sherlock Holmes stories, and Shakespeare.

He was a wonderful and engaging companion. However, his freedom had not made him a saint. He indulged his "weaknesses," as he put it, sometimes at the expense of others as he enjoyed his world.

Early on, one of this group, who had become a lawyer, had been called upon to bail him out of a Jamaican jail where he had been held for some time.

He joked that he had been instructed to bring a little extra money to ensure his extradition, a fresh dry-cleaned white shirt folded on a cardboard back the way he liked it, and pressed pants, because within a half hour of his release they would both be drinking Rémy Martin at a Jamaican bar.

We all knew Brad would not always be so lucky. He spent almost three years in Fox Hill prison in Nassau, and a year and a half imprisoned in Morocco, but it was the independence in him that we chose to remember.

No one knows for sure how he died.

He always had enemies in the trade, but he had also made good money doing commercial fishing off the New England coast. He disappeared offshore in the Atlantic during a squall off Cape Cod.

Nothing was ever found of him or his boat.

All the sailors in the conversation agreed that to leave no flotsam or jetsam behind was highly unusual.

The conversation turned from a general discussion of the squall to jokes about how improbable it was that the squall was really his cause of death.

Someone chimed in about how Brad had one time taken his boat to ride out a hurricane off Florida because being tied up at a dock would be riskier. However, when he had returned afterward, there were footprints on the ceiling of the cabin because his boat had rolled completely over during the storm.

Another friend suggested it was more likely that Brad had been hit by a freighter on the commercial trade routes that never saw him. Others who knew him well believed it was a settlement of old scores by others, and he had died with an anchor around his neck and his boat had been dragged back, repainted, and was now repurposed somewhere on the inland waterways, probably down south.

"No," one of them chimed in. "He's alive in Hawaii free of his enemies and debts." One friend laughed as he peeled off toward the bar. "If he was alive, he would be here. He is the bride's godfather. Remember how he had come to her high school graduation in a white suit? He took this stuff seriously!"

It is funny how old bonds of real friendship never break and how, when you see an old friend's face, the young face can be reconstructed from a familiar smile or a remembered look. It is both a resurrection from the past and rebirth into the future.

Brad is still forever young for us even now, 50 years later, as we are for each other.

My Effort to Avoid Thinking About American Politics

In my effort to avoid thinking about American politics, I found myself daydreaming about years ago when I was sitting in a bar in the night markets of Bangkok, Thailand, drinking a scotch...

Obviously, I was working hard to avoid thinking about American politics.

... The night markets sold everything and then disappeared at dawn. For some reason, as I sat in the bar drinking, I was thinking about people who collect things: art, old stamps, fine wine, or antique books.

Several days before, I had been up north in Chiang Mai and had decided I wanted to buy an antique Buddha statue. I was informed that it was illegal to take an antique Buddha statue out of Thailand, and the penalty could include jail time. I had no real interest in art, old stamps, fine wine or antique books, and antique Buddha statues could only be viewed by scholars or museum staff.

However, there was a black market, and I wanted adventure.

I asked around and was told there was a back room in a small store in the outskirts of the city. I booked a cab.

When I got to the store, I poked around and looked at the various objects that were for sale and eventually introduced myself to the owner. I innocently asked if he had any Buddhas I could see. He tried to interest me in a miniature figure that was in a partially open box with little hinges that he assured me was from Angkor Wat. I demurred with a polite shrug, implying I thought it might not be genuine and repeated my inquiries about a Buddha.

After some questioning, he took me to the back of the store and threw aside a hanging sheet that acted as a door into a room with perhaps six or seven tables, each of which had several Buddhas placed on them.

I could see that several were extremely old. I had read up on the different historic influences and style changes over time and pointed out that these statues were from different places and times throughout Asia. But I was bluffing and flattering the proprietor. Out of my depth and about to be caught, I claimed to not understand because of language barriers. I kept the conversation going by asking questions.

I innocently asked what the cost would be to purchase one in particular. The proprietor at first brushed off the question, but I feigned innocence and kept asking until he pulled out his calculator and we were translating bots into dollars. Very quickly, I realize that the cost was way beyond what I could afford and smuggle out of the country.

Over the next week, I went into northern Laos and was crossing a bridge over a large river gorge. As I reached the other side, there was a street vendor with a little cart that was full screwdrivers, clips of all kinds, and knickknacks — as well as two beautifully carved opium pipes, which I think were fashioned out of water buffalo horns. I negotiated politely and purchased them for a few dollars.

Because I bought both pipes, I considered myself instantly a collector. I was exceedingly proud of myself.

When I returned to Chiang Mai on my way home, I asked the cab driver if he knew where I could buy a really beautiful antique opium pipe, and he dropped me off at an antique store that was mainly filled with beautiful furniture but there was a display case with several elegant opium pipes.

I asked if they had been used and he nodded affirmatively, because the soldiers in Chiang Kai-shek's army were sometimes paid with opium and these pipes had been used by the senior officers. He held them up so I could smell the sweet smell of the old smoke.

They were all beautiful. I bought one for around $30 and was also provided with all the operational equipment that went with it, except of course for the opium. He also had a book printed in English about the antique opium pipes, which I bought to round out my new collection.

During this trip, along with the opium pipes, I had collected gifts for others such as fabrics, articles of clothing, and the mandatory t-shirts, costume jewelry, and trinkets, which I packed in my big suitcase for storage on my way home.

After a long flight, with a brief stop in Frankfurt, all was good until they passed out customs forms and announced that we were close to our destination, Washington DC.

A horrible lightning bolt of realization shot through my body.

I was bringing into the country three used opium pipes, as well as the paraphernalia, and they were not in my carry-on bag, so I couldn't abandon the pipes and paraphernalia in the bathroom before we landed.

I was going to have to go through customs with them.

I was terrified.

As my terror ripened, I thought about the headlines in the newspaper about my airport arrest and the announcement of my disbarment.

My stupidity rolled over me like a dump truck, then it got worse when I started thinking about my prison sentence.

The plane started to descend. I had to think fast.

After thinking fast, I came up with, "I actually bought them for the Baltimore Museum of Art."

Maybe not.

Maybe just confess and go into full tears?

Maybe not!

I started feverishly filling out the customs form and reporting each and every piece of fabric, each and every article of clothing, and the mandatory t-shirts, costume jewelry and trinkets to try to fill up space until I recorded at the very end, "ceremonial pipes."

Maybe not!!!

I thought maybe they would let me go home because Bowie is a Scottish name and so I must be bringing in bagpipes...

I had abandoned reality.

The reentry line at customs was long as we each opened our bags and the officers routed through them. What else could they be looking for on a plane coming in from Asia other than drugs?

When my turn came, as the officer started going through my list and asked me in detail about each of the fabrics, articles of clothing, and the mandatory t-shirts, costume jewelry, and trinkets on my custom form, he instructed me to unzip my bag.

I saw his handcuffs and thought about being led away. Then the officer stopped and said, "Welcome back," and indicated that I should rezip my bag and move on.

I started a slow motion run as I pulled my bag behind me and blasted through the automatic doors into the airport. I saw the car that was to pick me up. I saw the driver waiting for me with my name on a sign as I moved in slow motion toward him.

Then I had an entirely inappropriate emotion. I was so cool! I was a drug king pin evading capture but then... then, as I made it through the automatic doors into the airport, to my right I saw a police officer walking a sniffing dog!

I definitely was not a drug kingpin!

I didn't look twice. I just focused on my name on the card, which the driver was holding. I threw my arms out toward him as if he were a close relative or personal friend who I had not seen in a long time, or like some photo shoot for a Hallmark card, even though the object of my affection was an old geezer holding my name on a card who had no idea who I was.

I dropped my bags by the car, and somehow avoided the deep need to kiss him. The police officer and the dog moved on.

The driver put my bag in the trunk and, as he opened the door for me, I thought, "Well, damn it. It's too early for a double scotch."

Learning to Live Rather than Litigate

Recently, as I waited to exit a Southwest flight in Baltimore, a fellow traveler — who also turned out to be a fellow retired lawyer — laughed and asked me whether retirement had changed my life much, or perhaps had even changed my view of humanity.

The two of us had met and decided to sit together in the Boston airport while waiting to board from positions A-1 and A-2 for business class seating.

Now we both were waiting patiently to exit from the middle of the plane because the 22 wheelchair-assistance passengers who had preboarded would be exiting from their aisle seats, which they had taken when they entered the plane.

I decided to answer the two questions separately. First, I told a brief story to illustrate what my life was like as a practicing lawyer:

One afternoon around four o'clock while I was actively practicing law years ago, I developed chest pains. I was on the phone with a witness for an upcoming trial, so I decided that I would finish the call before I dealt with the pain in my chest.

After the call, I decided to try hanging off a door to ease the pain.

I found a door that was part open, put my hands on the top, and hung from the door to see if the pain would go away. After a while it did, so I went back to work.

Later that night at dinner with my wife and children, the pain returned. I didn't want to trouble anybody, so I left the dinner table, found a door and hung off of it for a bit until the pain subsided again. Then I flushed the toilet for cover and went back to dinner.

But later, around 1:00 a.m., the pain returned. I got out of bed to find an open door somewhere in the house. My wife woke up, rolled over, and saw me hanging from the bedroom door. She told me to go immediately to the hospital.

However, when I went into the closet to get dressed, the only clean shirt that was readily available was a white shirt just back from the dry cleaner. I put it on and looked for a pair of pants. I found only a suit, which I immediately put on and then I was stuck with a problem. I couldn't possibly go in a white shirt without a tie, so I just reached into the rack of ties and put on the first one I grabbed. I didn't turn on the light because I didn't want to wake up the house, so I didn't even know what color it was.

Finally, I got lucky. I had no problem tying the tie in the dark.

It was about 2:00 a.m. and the roads were empty as I sped down the highway toward the nearest hospital. The pain was getting pretty bad and for the first time it occurred to me I might die.

In that moment in the dark, my mortality became very real to me. I concluded I might never leave the hospital.

It was a remarkable revelation for me, so I reached into the glove compartment and pulled out what I considered would probably be my last cigarette.

At the emergency room parking lot, I started to get out of the car, but realized that my briefcase was in the passenger seat next to me. I was concerned that there were confidential papers belonging to my client pertaining to the trial that were in that briefcase so I brought the briefcase with me into the emergency room and politely let the nurse know that I was having chest pains.

Before I knew what was happening, I was being pushed back into the seat of a wheelchair with my briefcase squarely riding on my lap and then wheeled at a high rate of speed toward cardiac care by a nurse in the night time hospital. She patted me on the shoulder and asked in an exasperated voice, "So you think you might have a heart attack at two-thirty in the morning and be back at the desk by seven?"

My new friend laughed.

"Luckily, it wasn't a heart attack," I told him. "It was just gallstones that nearly killed me. I think the nurse overreacted."

"Maybe," he smiled. "It's all how you look at things."

As my story ended, we began to move down the aisle and exited the plane. Gathered by the gate were almost 20 wheelchairs. None of them had been used to take any of the passengers into the airport.

My traveling companion and I both laughed good-naturedly. "So, what about my second question," he prompted. "Has your view of humanity changed?"

"It's all how you look at things," I replied with a wry smile. "Isn't it wonderful that Southwest doesn't charge extra for miracles?"

We laughed and hurried to our next transportation.

Friends & Family

Photo: Joe Shlabotnik

Dancing School

For my friends and me, life was abruptly changed on the after school athletic fields in the spring of our eighth-grade year, when all of our parents signed us up for dancing school. My friends and I were all told it was a non-negotiable part of our education.

We were divided on the subject until one of us confessed that in church he had recently prayed to God that he be allowed to live long enough to experience sex. We found this to be reasonably compelling and it was sufficient to open the door for the rest of us to give in and accept the inevitable.

We had been given no previous training for this.

My preparation for dancing school was to wash my hair and then soap and rinse myself several times until I was squeaky clean, then do pull ups on the shower curtain rail in front of the mirror until I began to perspire and couldn't do anymore, in order to improve my physique.

Dancing school started at 4:30 p.m. It was held in the middle school cafeteria at our all-boys day school. After lunch, all the tables were moved to one side, the chairs were placed side by side along opposite walls, and a piano was rolled into place.

Our instructors, Mr. and Mrs. Knot, were a husband-and-wife team who appeared to be in their 30s. The husband played the piano, smoked constantly, and showed no enthusiasm. We all liked him from the start.

His wife however was stern, and dressed in black high heels and a low-cut black dress that featured her remarkable figure. From the start we had a problem. We couldn't look at her, but we couldn't take our eyes off of her.

Mrs. Knot would single out the tallest boy to dance with her. She would teach him the steps while the rest of us watched. We were then lined up with the girls from tallest to shortest and we could repeat their example.

Mrs. Knot soon showed the boys how they could politely change partners on the dance floor by tapping a boy on the shoulder.

One of the shortest boys in the class, who had big glasses, tapped Mrs. Knot's dance partner on the shoulder in what appeared to be a shameless attempt to gain favor with his teacher. She appeared to approve, until they began to dance and she realized that her high heels and his height had placed his nose in her cleavage and his glasses were focused squarely on her breasts.

The girls were at least a head taller than most of the boys and, after a week or two, Mrs. Knot announced a "ladies' choice."

The ladies' choice turned out to be an extremely athletic event. The girls were choosing boyfriends, but we didn't know that.

They would slowly stand and walk toward their target, but if there was competition, they would pick up the pace and start running. There were times when two competitors, in an effort to get their boy and also to stop, would pile up and slide under the chairs where we were sitting.

The situation grew more mature. Later that spring, I had a girlfriend for almost a month, but I didn't know that until she dumped me.

This was not unusual. Attachments were formed and broken in many cases before a boy even knew he had been going steady.

I was in my second relationship and didn't know it until I was informed that it was over. I was told by a girl who I didn't know that I had just broken up with a girl and that I was now available.

As the classes drifted into spring, the more adventurous girls would talk their parents into parties in the basement of their home.

They were all pretty much the same. They featured a record player and rotating chaperones to make sure nobody danced close during "Moon River." The rule was stiff-arm dancing with visible open space between the dancers.

As the spring finished up, the chaperones and other parents migrated upstairs and gathered in the living room for cocktails. Occasionally, they would do sneak attacks or peek down into the basement to make sure the lights had not been dimmed or turned off and people were not dancing close to "Moon River." They always claimed they were just making sure "the snacks had not run out."

By summer, we had made friends with girls and even fallen in love and knew it.

Something beautiful had happened that spring. Nobody really knew what it was other than a transition, but it was beautifully woven together as a rite of passage for everyone, including the parents.

The following spring, as upper-school ninth graders, we would spill out of school at 4:30 p.m. and look in the windows of the cafeteria as Mrs. Knott waltzed her way through another dumbfounded eighth-grade class.

We had friends that were girls now, and we even knew enough to know we had girlfriends. I had even learned to do pull ups before the shower.

Our Culture as the Hands of a Sculptor

The culture we live in is like the hands of a sculptor.

Because of undiscovered learning issues, it took me six years to get through high school. I had to repeat fourth grade, ninth grade and 11th grade and, of course earlier, I attended summer schools.

Because I moved from school to school a bit, I came to learn that the classrooms taught us very little compared to the culture of the schools where we were taught.

All of these schools had very different cultures.

After my first ninth grade at a day school, I was shipped to a boarding school in western Connecticut for my second attempt. I was a 16-year-old ninth grader.

I was embarrassed about my age and kept it secret because many of the other ninth graders were almost two years younger. I was bigger than many of the ninth-grade students and I inadvertently made the varsity soccer team.

The only other ninth grader who made the varsity soccer team was young for the ninth grade and was small, a little overweight, and had been appointed the manager of the team. His job was to keep track of the soccer balls and pack up uniforms for away games.

Let's call him PG. PG and I were both outcasts for different reasons. I think he was the only Jewish student at this boarding school and I was the only 16-year-old ninth grader. PG was very funny, with a self-mocking sense of humor once he let you know him, and he was as nice as he could be.

From the start, all the seniors and juniors on the varsity soccer team picked on PG. At the end of every practice, they would kick the balls in different directions to see if PG would miss dinner. Because we were both ninth graders, I would join him to collect the soccer balls.

A certain amount of this practice of cruelty was leveled at him because he was Jewish and small, so his persecution became the basis of a tribal unity not only for the soccer team but the school.

This was part of the culture of the school.

The faculty member who organized dances with girls' schools chose by grade-level, seniors first. I got to go in place of shorter sophomores because I was taller. We lined up and were matched with our date from tallest to shortest. The faculty member told me to tell my date that I was in 11th grade.

It was all about appearances.

The cruelty ran both ways. The boys nicknamed the faculty member "grave digger" because he had been a mortician in the army, saw himself as a southern aristocrat, and had a huge Adam's apple.

The most important event each day happened after the first two classes, when recess allowed people to go to their mailboxes and get mail from girls. The girls were also imprisoned in boarding schools and they would perfume their letters. The more perfumed letters you got the more your status grew.

I got perfumed letters, but PG, because he was small and younger, was not invited to those dances and did not get perfumed letters.

PG's mistreatment was relentless and included rolled wet towels to make "rat tails," which would be snapped in the locker rooms and at one point caused a bleeding cut on PG's leg.

One awkward boy got an erection in the shower and was dutifully punished with a rat tail.

PG suffered his indignities with great courage and, even though we were in different dorms, we at least knew each other and knew we liked each other.

The administration obviously knew what was happening, but they did nothing other than let the tribalism run wild.

They were letting boys become men.

I saw one boy get expelled from school. Right after recess the headmaster (the title back then) knocked on the door as the class was settling down.

When he entered, he addressed one fellow in the back row. He said he wanted to talk to the boy. The boy got up, took two steps toward the door, and the headmaster looked at him and said, "bring your books."

After PG had made no team sport during the winter's sports schedule, and also had made no team in the spring — each time treated badly as the manager for one team or another — he quietly gave up.

Just before recess that spring, after the spring teams had been chosen, the fire alarm went off and no one was allowed to leave their classrooms to go down to the mailboxes.

The sounds of an ambulance and a firetruck could be heard coming down the little road that ran beneath the windows of our third-floor classroom.

The teacher pulled down the shades.

After about a half an hour, we heard the sirens leave and we were released from class. Everyone went down to the mailboxes except me. I waited until the classroom was empty and then I pulled the shade up and peaked out the window.

Two maintenance men were hosing down a place three floors below the window, and the water was emptying down the road into a sewer. The water was blood red.

At lunch, the headmaster asked for a moment of silence because an accident had happened. He announced that PG had fallen off the fifth-floor roof of the classroom building. After that, there were no updates about PG and his injuries.

Several times thereafter, I went to the nurse's office and asked where I could send a card to PG. I was politely discouraged. Finally, after more visits, the nurse told me, in strict confidence, a secret. I was told that PG had jumped headfirst off the roof and had died on impact.

The students who succeeded at that school were like all good kids, but the culture was defined by tribal safety at the expense of others. Its viciousness rewarded its members with confidences that weren't kept and conspiracies that were suspect. It was about "me" not "us."

PG was real and the school killed him, but he took the souls of the living with him when he died.

Midway thought the next year, the headmaster knocked on the door after recess as we were settling in to class and encouraged me to bring my books.

He took me to my dorm room and I loaded my belongings into two suitcases. By the time it was lunchtime, I was at the Springfield bus station headed home.

I think of PG and believe we are better than this.

The culture we live in is like the hands of a sculptor.

The Older You Get the Shorter Your Stories Should Be

Photo: Tom Swift

More and More These Days I Find Myself Waiting for the Answering Machine

When I was a kid people didn't die, they just became invisible and didn't answer the phone.

One of those disappearances for me was my friend Haven Story. He's a little different, though, because after a couple of decades, I still believe he lost his phone and will return my calls when he finds it.

This scenario was always more likely because he appeared to be indestructible, like he had been gifted with nine lives.

You pretty much could always count on updates about him getting to you before he did. I heard one time when he was in New York City, he hitched a ride with the trash truck to get to his next party.

One night in the late '60s or early '70s, we were at a party that was wrapping up somewhere around three or four in the morning when he made a troubling but carefully considered announcement:

"I think we have run out of thrills!"

He looked around and put his smoking cigar into an empty beer bottle as he reached for a phonebook.

"But I have an idea! We've got to go skydiving — right now!"

About an hour away in Orange, Massachusetts, there was a skydiving operation that would open for the day somewhere around 10 o'clock in the morning.

Without hesitation, we piled into the car, drove into the night, parked in the parking lot, and slept for a few hours. We were there when it opened.

There were four of us who sat in the classroom as they explained what we would do and what would happen. The instructor laid out a parachute and packed it so it would open when the ripcord was pulled. We were also given an emergency parachute which we were told we should "punch, pull and flap like a towel to catch the air as we were falling."

Haven was always animated in whatever he was doing. He had an endless sense of humor as he engaged with the world. He used his hands to express the enormity of his thoughts.

Wide-eyed with excitement, he was ready to jump. He wanted to be at the head of the line and first to jump as we entered the plane.

The plane was a big cargo transport plane with enough room for about 20 jumpers. We sat on benches with our ripcords buckled to the plane above our heads.

Our target was a huge sandbox 3,000 feet below. After calculating the wind speed, the plane circled so that when we jumped the wind would generally take us in the direction of the sandbox. Then we were instructed: "Jump now!"

The instructor was on the ground with a walkie-talkie. He could give us instructions after the chute opened so that we could guide ourselves with his help to our "tuck and roll," which minimized the impact of our landing.

Haven went first out the door with an unabashed scream of joy into the free fall until his shoot opened and he reached up to the toggles to navigate his way down.

I, a little more reluctantly, jumped next and fell into the tumult of wind until my chute opened, I reached up and grabbed my toggles, and found myself involuntarily swinging my feet far above the ground, observing the earth and its fields, rooftops, and intersecting highways before focusing on the upcoming sand landing.

It was an overwhelming moment. A mix of fear and exhilaration.

I saw Haven land and tuck and roll and stand up immediately and start jumping up and down as I stretched my feet out and prepared to land.

Haven ran to meet me with his chute dragging behind him. His eyes wide his arms flailing around him. He grabbed me and said "Let's do it again! Let's do it again! Wooooooooooow! Let's do it again!"

We really couldn't say no. The four of us jumped three more times that day.

I miss Haven.

I think I'll try him on the phone one more time.

Once Upon a Time I Had the Darwin Award Snatched from My Grasp

In a previous post, I wrote about my first parachute jump with my wonderful and crazy lost friend Haven.

But here is the rest of the story...

About ten years after my jumps with Haven, I told the story during lunch at the law firm where I worked.

As I finished, a few members of the staff and two associates unexpectedly got up and left. They came back about 10 minutes later with an announcement.

There was a parachute place on the Eastern Shore of Maryland just across the Bay Bridge, about two hours away and, if I wasn't a coward or just a B.S. storyteller, they would go next Saturday with me. But only if I would do the first jump.

That night, my wife just shook her head, looked at me in disbelief and said, "At least you don't have any children."

Because of my luncheon bravado, I was now a fool following myself down a path I did not want to follow... but it got worse.

The following Saturday, eight of us piled into two cars and drove down to "Parachutes Are Fun," which looked a lot different than the professional business in Massachusetts where I first jumped.

Parachutes Are Fun featured one single engine plane with all the seats removed except for the pilot's, a barn, and a school bus that had no tires and was up on cinder blocks.

As if launched from the bus, an overly excited prematurely aged young man with wild blond hair and dilated pupils approached us. He looked like a stunt double for the old guy in *Back to the Future*. He held a helmet in one hand and a lit cigarette in the other and couldn't stop welcoming us even before we got out of the car.

At the same time, the owner came out of the barn, dressed in a bombardier's jacket with Parachutes Are Fun stenciled on the back, carrying a walkie-talkie. Behind him was as an assistant leading four people with parachutes on their backs to the little plane as a pilot in blue jeans, a baseball hat and sneakers was entering the cockpit of the plane.

This was way too informal! This was not good.

It was too late to change directions and forever be the coward who turned around and for once in his life had been responsible.

We were divided into two groups of four based solely on the car in which we came, and I was volunteered to be in the group that would jump first.

The character from the bus enthusiastically showed us how he packed the parachutes and couldn't stop promoting as he did. He was excited to tell us he lived in the bus and loved his job so much that he took his raises and bonuses in free jumps.

Our new friend who lived in the bus took off with every plane and was responsible for everything from our chutes being packed properly to cursory instructions about the emergency chute if the primary shoot "perhaps" didn't open, as well as coordinating the open door jumps from the plane that had taken off as we had entered.

As the plane circled overhead, the owner turned on his walkie-talkie and watched as the first diver spreadeagled at about 2,500 feet above us.

The chute opened and the owner barked into the walkie-talkie, "Pull your left toggle"... "Reach up and PULL YOUR LEFT TOGGLE," and then turned to the assistant and yelled, "That son of a bitch loaded them in in the wrong order again, dammit! I'm talking to somebody who hasn't jumped yet!"

The clueless diver was drifting, arms at his side, downwind at a high rate of speed toward northern Virginia.

The owner shoved his hand into his pocket, threw a set of car keys to the assistant and told him, "Follow the bastard and pick him up where he lands!" Three jumps later, the plane taxied down the dirt road runway to the barn to reload as the jumpers landed helter-skelter in the surrounding soybean fields.

I concluded this chaos was all a very good sign.

I had strategically decided to show no fear and thus as the others saw the disorder around them, the fear would gather in them and they would decide to go home. But when I finally decided to make eye contact in preparation for supporting their decision, I was shocked to find that they didn't have a clue because they thought all this was normal.

Before I knew it, I was on the plane sitting on the floor next to the open door as we took off. It didn't help me to feel any better that I could hear the guy with the walkie-talkie in communication with the assistant as he tried to follow a parachute in his car, zigzagging through highways and byways while trying to keep his eye on a disappearing spot in the sky. I considered the children and family I would never have.

I am vain enough to not ride roller coasters because I don't want that as the cause of death in my obituary. As we rose higher and higher in the sky and waited to jump, I decided I wanted to be remembered, if at all, as the fearless, selfless, courageous parachutist who had advised the other three jumpers who would jump after him that if by some chance the walkie-talkie failed they could pull the toggles to face the wind in order to drop slowly straight down rather than have their backs to the wind and end up dead in some unfamiliar state.

The following week, late one afternoon, two of the people who had jumped with me came into my office laughing and holding *The Evening Sun*.

They had five copies open to a series of pictures and a headline that read, "Eastern Shore's 'Parachutes Are Fun' Shut Down as America's Most Dangerous!" There were several pictures of skydivers stranded on rooftops or hanging from high tension wires, as well as a beaming portrait of our friend who had just been evicted from the bus.

Slowly, as I reach maturity and a belief in evolution, I thank God for my children and grandchildren and that their mother's DNA has prevailed.

The Older You Get the Shorter Your Stories Should Be

About Dizlxia

Here's the thing about Dizlxia... sorry. Dicklessia... Dilexsia... sorry.

BBC Science Focus Magazine, dated June 24th, 2022, headlined that researchers at Cambridge University have determined:

"Dyslexia isn't a disorder, it's part of our species' cultural evolution..."

This is wonderful news.

Apparently, I was part of a "cultural evolution" when I was flunking first-year Spanish three years in a row.

It wasn't because dyslexia was my "disorder." It must have been my "unconscious commitment to a cultural evolution."

That explains everything!

Maybe I have been creating my own language as part of this cultural evolution? Maybe English is my foreign language?

All these years, I haven't been some old dyslexic with a nasty addiction to spellcheck. Hell, no! I see myself differently now.

I'm sort of an old professor working and creating in my own language based on bad grammar, worse punctuation, and horrible misspellings! A pop artist working in a collage of words!

This is great! I have already contacted my old middle school and my four high schools and I have asked for a reevaluation.

I have asked that my grades be changed from F- to A+ because of my deep and abiding early commitment to being part of a cultural evolution, as is evident from the fact that I repeated 4th, 9th, and 11th grade and attended endless summer schools.

Because it took me six years to get through high school, after rereading the article, I requested masters' degrees from my past schools.

In hindsight, I jumped the gun. I should have asked for Ph.Ds.

What if this "cultural evolution" is the new age of honesty and fairness and we are all part of it?

I will confess in all honesty it came easily for me to create my own language (and at times even my own alphabet) but once I finally accepted that nobody could understand anything I wrote, it seemed fair because I couldn't understand anything they wrote either.

Anyway, because of this — my new linguistic and cultural understanding — I decided to give my new language a name. After all, it is not French or Spanish or Russian, no.

I decided to call it "BOB."

Despite what you think I did not name my language after myself. I named it BOB as a public service.

It is a language which is specifically designed for dyslexics because you can spell it frontwards or backwards and it is still B-O-B.

Let me give you an example:

B-O-B. You see? There I spelled it backwards.

The article went on to state:

"People with dyslexia have brains that are specialized to explore the unknown, and this strength has contributed to the success and survival of our species."

Wow! I am feeling blessed that I have "contributed to the success and survival of our species," because I am pretty certain that I have spent my whole life exploring the unknown.

When it takes six years to get out of high school it is not unreasonable to be exploring and expecting a long professional life in footwear.

Please read the *BBC Science Focus* magazine article to see if it applies to you.

It's not long. It's just about four, maybe five pages.

It only took me two months. If it takes you less don't worry about it.

It's a little different being part of cultural evolution, but it can be fun and it will teach you tons of empathy for other people.

Maybe that's the "cultural evolution" they are talking about. Even though we are all different we are all in this together.

Calling the Chickens Home

My mother was a quiet country girl. Even in the suburbs, she used the exact same whistle that her mother used to call the chickens when she wanted us home for dinner.

She married a strict but loving patriarch and had two sons. The three males all believed they were the center of the universe. When she died almost 15 years ago, she left an unexpected void in her place.

The three men she left behind slowly came to recognize she had been our gravity. I don't think I could have understood her while she was still alive. I think she knew that.

The year she died, she gave me a large steamer trunk, which she told me she had filled with the flotsam and jetsam of my very "learning disabled" childhood. She told me she had saved everything, beginning with kindergarten through when I passed the bar exam and she pronounced I was on my own, "because finally you will never have to take another test again."

It had been our war, which we fought side by side, against a world eager to write me off, forget me, marginalize me and perhaps us. Because I did not wish to return to that nightmare, I was never ready to open that box.

My mother had no fear of time. She had endless patience.

Because we lived in a patriarchy, we knew all about our family name, with its politicians, governors, distinguished lawyers, and Maryland history. But my mother's family of farmers and merchants on the Eastern Shore of Maryland with its southern roots was rarely discussed.

The year before she died in her mid-90s, she asked me to drive her down to Church Hill, Maryland, where her family of Chapmans, Valiants, and Faithfuls were buried around a small church in an agrarian tidewater town. She said she wanted me to see where she had come from. She had already given me the box by then.

As I recuperated from surgery over the last few weeks, I kept looking at that box. Last Sunday, I opened it.

As I gently pulled back the wrapping paper, I was surprised to find more than I expected. There were pictures of her relatives and ancestors who I had never really known. On the back were the names and dates and a few sentences about who they were and how they connected to my mother and our family. As I put the pictures up on the table and found them staring back at me, her life slowly formed around her in a way that included me.

I noticed that I looked like them more than I looked like my father's family.

Her father loved poetry and the arts. He had been a choral master and led singing groups and church choirs up and down the Eastern Shore of Maryland. There was a beautiful hand-crocheted bed cover, and a white embroidered tablecloth made by her mother, and more pictures of her two older brothers whom I barely knew.

At the very bottom, piled in chronological order and bound by a rubber band that had long since broken, were all of my teachers' reports. They started with kindergarten reports of a joyous, adventurous, somewhat shy little boy who the teachers found "amazing in his creativity and interest in the world," until the alphabet and reading and spelling were introduced in first grade and then the failures compounded year after year, as that little boy fell further behind, repeating grades or advancing to the next grade only if he would go to summer school, then encouraged to leave and go to another school, and ultimately to be told he could not go to college.

My mother was patient. My mother had no fear of time. She got me to dictate stories to her as I thrashed on the bed in the vacant third-floor room. She got me to write poems.

Each day after school, she made it her business to read all of my homework assignments to me as we curled up in a window seat, the afternoon sun pouring in through the windows. It didn't really help, but it was all she could do and she refused to give up on her disappointing son who was always falling behind.

My mother had no fear of time. She had endless patience.

We were all too self-centered to ever recognize who she really was. We all loved her, that was never an issue. But I am now convinced that when she went off to church alone on Sundays, that was something more than her quiet time.

After I spent better than a day with everything spread out on the dining room table, I finally closed the empty trunk. It had been a time bomb to be opened when I could finally understand it. It was an explosion.

Over the years, my father and my brother grew to realize that she had a unique relationship with each of us that was powerful and the source of the gravity that brought us all together. The trunk did not hold the history of my failure as I had thought it did. It held the history of our love as it had matured with faith and quiet determination, year after year, growing strong despite life's pressure.

My mother was patient. She had no fear of time.

She waited until I found a voice outside of failure, my family history. She trusted I would find that voice and make it my own. She waited until I found the arts in her family and in me. She waited until last Sunday to be more fully recognized.

Just Out of Reach

In a previous post, I wrote about my mother and how my grandmother would whistle her chickens home long ago on a farm on the Eastern Shore of Maryland and how my mother, not quite so long ago, used the same whistle to call her children.

My grandmother was the only grandparent I would know. She lost her husband and the farm when my mother was still in high school.

Even though we always lived far apart I remember as a small child feeling our inexplicable mutual affection when I would wish her happy birthday or Merry Christmas each year over the telephone.

Both my grandmother and my mother had a kindness that children almost intuitively recognized as safe.

While the schools taught reading, writing, arithmetic, and how to compete in the modern world, my mother and grandmother's universe was quite the opposite. It was more gentle. They focused on the wellbeing of those they loved. Their world was often damage control.

I was lucky to have known them.

In fourth grade the family moved back to Boston from Washington, and I started my 4th new school in four years. That summer I had developed a temperature of 104° and was taken from Randolph,

New Hampshire down to Mass General hospital to see Dr. Gross, a specialist in children's lung problems.

The lower lobe of my left lung was removed which delayed my entrance into a new fourth grade class in which I would already be far behind because of the learning issues that had followed me from Washington.

The following summer I had to meet with tutors every day in order to be bumped up to the fifth grade. I had finally given up on school and slowly started to recess into myself and my gathering emotional despair.

In August, I got a break from the tutoring before fifth grade started.

The next thing I knew, I was scheduled to visit my grandmother in Chestertown, MD for the first time.

My grandmother was in her early 70s and lived alone in one of two small apartments on the 4th floor in an old building next to the bridge over the Chester River, which brought slow moving cars and rattling trucks in and out of Chestertown.

That first evening together, we ate a simple dinner on the card table. Then we went down the fire escape to the backyard with a jar with ice pick holes for air in its tin screw top to catch lightening bugs. Later, when the lights were out, they would be let loose in my room.

Like her daughter, Granny — which is what she wished to be called — had the softest paper-thin skin as she aged but maintained rough dishpan hands, which were perfect for back rubs.

I remember that first night being tucked into bed in an envelope of fitted sheets all alone in the darkness with the lightning bugs.

Somehow my tension disappeared into a quiet world that was my grandmother's domain.

The next morning, she vested me with adult authority. After an early breakfast of griddle cakes with maple syrup, grits, and kettle tea (kid's tea — milk and sugar but no teabag), it was unspoken but somehow understood that I would be carrying my side of the responsibility by doing the dishes.

At breakfast she planned our day. We would be walking into town to do her errands and I would buy a simple fishing pole, some hooks, a tin pail to hold a small pocket knife, extra lines, some worms, and a red bobber that would flip over and pop up if I got a bite from one of the catfish that the old men routinely pulled out of the Chester River from off the bridge.

Granny had this uncanny ability to create an adventure and treat it like the business of life. She told me not to bother the old men who were fishing but be nice to them if they talked to me.

The men left me alone, but they had stopped laughing together and focused on their fishing quietly as they occasionally looked over at me.

As I caught nothing, they caught several big catfish and I was envious. Slowly one of the men came over and asked if I would like some advice. I politely said yes and he pulled in my line, replaced my worm with bait from his pail, put on a sinker, and let the line drop into the brown water until it hit the bottom. Then he reeled it up so that the bobber would react to bites from where the catfish lived.

At the end of the day when everyone left the bridge, I left with them.

Midway through dinner, I proudly announced that I had made a friend. Without looking up, Granny asked, "Were you polite?" I assured her I was, which added to my sense of accomplishment, but I told her I did not catch any fish.

She said that she had done all the shopping that was necessary for our week, so I should be sure if I caught a fish to make sure that I gave it to my new friends. After dinner, and after I had done the dishes, because the sun had not yet gone down, we played slap jack on the folding table and I got pretty good at slapping jacks.

As the sun went down, we repeated our collecting of lighting bugs for the room, and the next morning I repeated the day before, but this time with a little more self-confidence. My grandmother told me to leave my windows open so the lightning bugs could rejoin their friends before the next upcoming night.

The men were already on the bridge when I walked up to join them with my pail and fishing rod, and they welcomed me. They clearly had been talking about me after I left them the day before.

I was proud that I had been polite and that they seemed to like me. Within an hour of meeting them, I caught a fish and it was pretty big. They showed me how to remove the hook from the big catfish's gaping mouth and I dropped it into one of the burlap bags.

The friendships increased into gentle humor, which was respectful on all sides but fun. That night we repeated the night before except my grandmother was laughing when I returned home, because she said that her downstairs neighbor had stopped her on the stairs to let her know that I had slapped a jack so hard the pendulum had come off of the grandfather clock in the apartment below.

I went back to school that fall and continued to fail, but I was less hesitant to call my grandmother just to talk but never to complain. We never talked about anything important, but somehow we did.

Later that year, my mother left Boston hurriedly one morning to go down to Chestertown and I grew worried but couldn't speak.

When I got home from school, my father was waiting.

I told him I was worried about my mother. I wanted to call my grandmother, but he took me into the living room and held both my hands and said, "You can't call her now. She has died."

That was well over 60 years ago. We would both be about the same age now.

Even now, there are still times when I feel that I want to call her, but somehow I can't seem to find the number.

The Older You Get the Shorter Your Stories Should Be

Photo: UAV 605 (olvwork369376). Harvard University Archives.

Learning to Accept Love

My father was born August 24th, 1909 and died November 2nd, 2013. Somehow my love and respect for him continues to grow. It happened over time, but it is much like what Mark Twain said:

"When I was a boy of 14, my father was so ignorant I could hardly stand to have the old man around. But when I got to be 21, I was astonished at how much the old man had learned in seven years."

Imagine how astonished I was by "the old man" after I had continued to witness his learning as he passed 100. He set the standard. He told me one time in my youth, "I love you, but I don't respect you." He was right. He was always razor sharp and I grew to want his respect.

He had been first in his class in everything he had ever done and could cut through the fog to get to the heart of an issue with a single lightning bolt comment, but the real reason I thought so highly of him was I saw him choose to live with determined integrity.

During the last 15 years of his life, he lived in a retirement home near where I worked. The other old men on his floor gave up shaving for weeks but I would always shave him before he would leave his room as my show of love and respect. I would visit him every afternoon and wheel him into dinner unless I was in a trial or out of town.

In the mid-1990s, in yet another effort to win his respect, I enthusiastically informed him that this new Internet thing would open us to world peace. He smiled and said, "probably not that easy." He was right and I was flat on my face again. I could only think of what he must have thought of me in my teens during the "don't trust anybody over 30" period.

I was the worst kid ever. I had undiscovered learning issues back then, and well-developed disciplinary problems. I kept getting thrown out of school and — to make things worse — I would disappear to hitchhike through at least 40 of the states.

One time when I was heading back to Maryland, I called home from a payphone in a Howard Johnson's south of Chicago because a driver who picked me up bribed me with food if I would call my parents to tell them that I was coming home. My mother answered the phone and could not stop crying because she said she had been so worried. Despite my misspent youth, my father and mother never gave up on me. I was their son despite my failures. They would do the right thing. That determined integrity was a commitment to love. I wanted to learn that.

One afternoon when he was 94, he complained of pains in his lower abdomen and after an ambulance ride to the hospital he was admitted to surgery.

As I prayed in an empty waiting room very late at night, I thought I was never going to see him alive again. On scratch paper I sketched out a sonnet of remembrance. I wrote it after they wheeled him out of the operating room.

My Father

In the end it's touch that holds memory.
The other senses are immediate
And defend the present territory.
The other four are there to navigate.

Tonight my father went under the knife
And I waited alone with my cell phone
To see what would become of this one life;
Together, separate, and both alone.

For an hour in the last waiting room,
I remembered him as sound and insight,
Too perspicacious for the cool boxed room
That would contain him in this, his last night.

At ninety-four how could he have survived?
I kissed the forehead of a man, alive.

As he approached his 100th birthday, we were talking and he, almost as an afterthought, said, "I admire what you have accomplished with your life. I'm not sure I could have done what you have done." I don't think he ever realized that was the one thing I had always hoped to hear from him. Our last years together were perfect. He had never withheld love. I just had refused to accept its responsibilities.

Shaving My Father
(From a draft I wrote the day after my father's death at 104.)

This is the last small room in which he will rest.
Every day I visit him at four o'clock.
We balloon the room with our forgiveness.
"Either this man is dead or my watch has stopped."

Two men knock on his door then wait like guests.
"Not funny for a man this close to death."
We share what only dark humor can express.
The Marx brothers, for both of us, are the best.

The electric razor hums in my hand
As it cuts along the cheekbone and the neck.
Like a harvester on pre-winter land
I harvest thistle from earth's intellect

Across a snow bank of thin paper skin.
They zip their bag shut and leave me without him.

People & Politics

An Offer and Acceptance

Last Friday, I skipped lunch and went back to my Boston hotel room to watch Congressman Elijah Cummings's funeral on TV.

Thirty-five years ago, when he was still a lawyer, we had a case together. I was representing a modular building company and he was representing one of the prominent African American churches in Baltimore, which had contracted with my client to buy and construct a building for Baltimore city primary school students.

Elijah and I met on the top floor of the church overlooking North Avenue where the ministers' offices were located. He came over, shook my hand, and said, "I do a lot of criminal law and you know a lot more about business law than I do. Can we agree to work to make this fair for both sides?" I shook his hand and agreed that would be our objective.

The contract negotiations and construction took some time. As the building went up, there were adjustments to the plans and "change orders," as there always are in construction cases, but we were candid with each other and each time we got it right.

Years later, I was at the Democratic convention in Boston and he saw me. Coming over with a big smile, he said: "Yeah! We learned to work well together, didn't we?" We both laughed.

I grew up in Cambridge, Massachusetts, and one of my favorite places is an old rusted fountain dedicated to John F. Kennedy. It no longer works but still has his quotes chiseled on its sides.

My hotel was in Harvard Square, so after the funeral I walk down to the fountain and read the quotes again:

"Today the eyes of all people are truly upon us — and our governments, in every branch, at every level, national, state, and local, must be as a city upon a hill — constructed and inhabited by men aware of their grave trust and their great responsibilities."

Next to the forgotten monument was a sign that said: "No Skateboarding."

No one was there except a skateboarder, practicing and re-practicing his art, and me.

It occurred to me that there are always laws which will be broken but we all, somehow, are subject to a deeper code. This was what Elijah understood.

Thousands of people, whether in the church or on TV, watched Elijah's funeral. They watched and listened and were there because Elijah was an example of something we seem to not be able to forget.

Although in our daily lives and in our politics and governance it is sometimes lost, it is there in that handshake, that eye contact, that second thought that reminds us that it is as constant as gravity.

I saw Elijah on and off after that, in airports or at campaign events. He had become my congressman. We would smile or wave. We were not friends, but we had once come to an understanding because he had offered up his vulnerability so that I could offer mine. And we could trust each other just long enough to do something right.

The Older You Get the Shorter Your Stories Should Be

I Almost Got the Chance to Cite the Constitution in Traffic Court

I remember when Congress actually had good manners and I almost got a chance to cite the Constitution in traffic court.

Many years ago, from within a culture of politeness, I watched the U.S. Congress impeachment proceedings of Richard Nixon. Now, 45 years later, this culture of politeness in Congress doesn't exist, but back then it seemed to have several benefits.

I got a job in the office of Senator Charles "Mac" Mathias (R-MD) as his mail clerk. My "office" was directly behind the wall that separated me from the receptionist and everybody else.

After several months, I got a chance to demonstrate my enthusiasm. The Senator knocked on my door and told me he had a "special assignment" for me.

He told me that there was a lobbyist right on the other side of that wall who was sitting in the receptionist area. The lobbyist had just threatened to pull all of his airline clients out of BWI unless the Senator voted in favor of a bill that would be considered by the Senate that afternoon.

The senator told me to take the lobbyist to the Senate dining room and take detailed notes on what he wanted.

I straightened my tie, went through the door, and introduced myself.

After a brief moment, the lobbyist looked me over and asked me, "What exactly is your job title?"

I proudly told him, "I am the mail clerk!"

He thanked me, declined my invitation to the Senate dining room, and left.

One of the benefits of this culture of politeness was it encouraged good manners without public reprimand.

The Senator eventually took pity on me and I became his driver.

Back then, the Senate was bipartisan and the senators got along. We filled up the back seat with the likes of Kennedy from Massachusetts and Tower from Texas. We all listened to the political news in the car together on WTOP.

Despite often radically different points of view, this civility grew from a collective belief that these representatives were exercising a shared power. It made sense. This responsibility of shared power allowed a culture of compromise and progress that we have not seen since the country has been polarized.

There was a reverence on both sides for the Constitution. Mathias always had a copy in his coat pocket.

No one was immune from this culture, including me. One time as we were headed to Washington from the western part of the state, Mathias leaned over to me, turned down the radio, and said, "We can pick it up a little. You are going to law school. If we get pulled over, you will be able to cite the Constitution to the officer." Mathias smiled as he patted his coat pocket. "It is illegal to hinder a member of Congress on the way to a vote."

I never asked him for the chapter and the verse. I just drove a little faster. It just made sense.

The Older You Get the Shorter Your Stories Should Be

It Is Different Now, but It Remains the Same

You can call it "fake news" or the subjugation of truth, but when confronted by self-serving diatribes and obstructionist partisan arguments, I saw several witnesses at the Nixon impeachment hearings persist and tell the truth — or at least preserve its credibility — no matter how difficult that was for them.

When I was a driver for U.S. Senator Charles "Mac" Mathias (R-MD) during the Watergate proceedings, news and politics were different than today. Credibility was everything.

On TV, Walter Cronkite delivered the truth on the CBS Evening News. He was voted the most trusted man in America.

The newspapers never had that power of personality, but they doggedly stood behind their stories, even when they relied upon undisclosed sources like "Deep Throat." They knew they were at risk every day.

Credibility sold the news, and advertising, and paid for heavy overhead and lots of investigative reporters.

Today, news sources on the web do not need credibility. They have followers instead.

They are also not at risk because they have few, if any, expenses and are often not even identifiable. Social media is flooded with unverifiable news sources, some of which are paid for by our enemies as they seek to disrupt our country's elections.

Senator Mathias was from Frederick, Maryland — farm country — two hours west of DC. He was fiercely loyal to his city and his state. He cherished his reputation for integrity and his nickname, "The Conscience of the Senate."

It was different back then, but it is still the same.

I was driving Mathias when he was summoned by President Nixon to an afternoon rally the next day. Mathias was to be filmed beside Nixon for the evening news that night. Mathias had, in essence, been summoned to give the President an unspoken endorsement in Maryland's Washington suburbs, in Mathias's home state.

Maryland is an overwhelmingly Democratic state. Mathias was no fan of Nixon and Nixon knew it, but Nixon was a Republican and so was Mathias.

Credibility was everything to Mathias, but he couldn't say "no" to the president without punishment from his party.

I picked the Senator up at his home that morning and we headed to his scheduled meetings.

The first thing he said to me as he got into the car was, "looks like that tread on the left rear tire is thin."

After the morning meetings and before lunch, I offered to take the car to get the tire checked, but Mathias said he wanted me inside to record his speech on the handheld tape recorder I always carried with me for such occasions. He made sure he was never misquoted.

After lunch, as he got into the car he pointed and asked me, "You think it looks like that tread is dangerous?"

I insisted that I get the tire checked immediately so we would be on time for the rally.

The Senator thought for a judicious moment. "I think you are right, Bob. Let's get it looked at." But as I turned into a filling station he quietly said, "I have always bought my tires up at the Goodyear store in Frederick."

By the time we got back to Washington, the rally was over. As I let him out of the car that night, he asked me to remind him to send his apologies to the White House.

To maintain credibility in the face of power, persistence may not always offer the opportunity to speak the truth. But at least it's a statement on its own: the resistance is a placeholder for the truth, and it retains our gravity.

It is different now, but it remains the same.

The Rebirth of the Heroes

After Ted Williams, Mohammed Ali and Bobby Orr, since I was a boy, I have been looking for heroes. There have been painfully few. The next generations have not, for me, been fertile ground.

I have just returned from a nine-day trip with a group of 15 friends through Mississippi, Arkansas, Alabama, and Tennessee. When I came home, I was shocked to learn of Alexei Navalny's murder in a Russian prison.

I remembered that after Putin tried to kill him once before, he returned to Russia, only to be imprisoned yet again and ultimately murdered. He risked everything for the love of his country, its people and an integrity that is larger than his life. That is this old man's kind of hero.

It wasn't my objective but on the trip, I accidentally found the heroes like Navalny that I have been looking for.

For years, I have wanted to follow the "nonviolent" civil rights movement from the death of Emmett Till in 1955 up to when the Rev. Dr. Martin Luther King, Jr. was killed in Memphis on April 4th, 1968.

Yes, I had seen all the pictures, read the books and knew the dates and places as we all have. This movement started when I was in lower school and compounded until it arguably ended with the assassination of Martin Luther King, Jr. when I graduated from high school in 1968.

It was all familiar to me.

But all the histories and research I had done became like reading the script of a play until I walked onto the stage where it had happened. Then I had no escape. It is different when you are surrounded by it. It is different when you become immersed in it.

The Delta blues surrounded us as we passed the crossroads where Robert Johnson is said to have sold his soul to the devil, then parked down the road near Baptist town to walk near where he had been laid to rest.

Much of the Mississippi Delta, our guide at the front of the bus informed us, is owned by eight families.

For hour after hour, the low flat land passes by, with row after row of cotton plants as far as the eye can see on both sides of the road.

Finally, we left the two-lane road from Jackson, Mississippi and traveled down a dirt road to a big house with five or six little cottages next door to it. These are the houses for the families of the tenant farmers who live there surrounded by their work, earning an annual income of around $8,000 a year — that is, before they paid their rent.

On the bus days later, I tried to better understand the famous 1957 photo of young Elizabeth Eckford as she tried to integrate Little Rock Central High School while screaming white people threatening her 67 years ago. Days later, I met her — now in her 80s — as she sat quietly in front of us and answered questions across from where it had all happened.

She said her parents were determined not to back down and they would not talk about it. She said it had taken her almost 40 years to come to grips with what had happened to her in that one day, and for the remainder of the school year, day after day, as she withstood catcalls and being shoved into lockers as she walked the halls.

That little girl in the picture with the sunglasses on, holding her books alone and determined, gives no evidence of the damage that was done to her, which had stayed with her for so long.

It was much the same with the picture I had seen of the cluster of black men in Memphis as they were all turning and pointing in unison as Martin Luther King, Jr. lay at their feet on the balcony of room 306 of the Lorraine Motel. The motel has been turned into a much bigger museum, with a plate glass wall preserving the room that these men had left to talk to friends three stories below. It is now forever frozen with the shades all drawn.

I was not ready for 14-year-old Emmett Till's final journey down from Chicago to visit family in Mississippi to the candy store where he whistled at a white girl. His two assassins had tracked him down three days later and extracted him at gunpoint from his relative's house to be beaten beyond recognition and dumped in the river. Days later, he was fished out to be buried back home in Chicago in an open casket.

It all rushed at me hours later, when I found myself in the courtroom where the two men were exonerated in 67 minutes by an all-white jury who said they had a ten-minute Coke break to extend the deliberations. I was sitting in the seat of juror number six, right across from the witness stand where Emmett's mother had testified in tears.

After I opened the news when I got home, Navalny's murder drove me back to that trip.

I found heroes in many of the locations we visited. In the Mississippi Civil Rights Museum, those heroes were in the records of the hundreds of lynchings, including many who could not be identified.

There are names we all remember, of course. They were committed to their country and to peaceful change despite the daily risk they might be killed. Martin Luther King, Jr., in his "I've Been to the Mountaintop" speech, said he could see the promised land, but perhaps he would not be there with them when they entered it. Soon thereafter, he was killed.

Medgar Evers, who was shot from across the street at midnight, had trained his children to run to the bathtub and hide whenever they heard gunshots, because it was the only place they might be safe from a high-powered rifle.

Medgar Evers was killed by a high-powered rifle bullet that went through him, through the front window of his living room, through the wall of his kitchen, and then lodged in the refrigerator.

These people died to advance the cause of freedom. Let's remember them as we move toward an election that could determine how free we really are.

The night I returned, after I unpacked and turned out the light and set the alarm for an early breakfast, I thought about the people who I had met and the surroundings that had given old history a new life. I went to sleep thinking of those people as little candles where I could warm my hands, little flickering lights burning in the dark.

Poets & Professors

Photo: Jane Reed/Harvard University

Yes, Love Grows Forever

I have been discovering that love grows over time with reflection.

In 1965, *Hogan's Goat*, a verse drama about love and politics set in turn-of-the-century Irish Brooklyn ran for over 600 performances on Broadway. It was written by Harvard Professor William Alfred, about the world in which he had grown up. In the early '70s it was made into a movie.

Alfred was a legend at Harvard. Everyone loved him because he was completely approachable, lived in unassuming rumpled clothes, and had a habit of giving all the change in his pocket to the street people in Harvard Square. He knew some of them by name.

As a teacher, he was beloved because he taught an unbelievably good class on Beowulf, old English, and poetry in Sanders Theater every year to well over 500 adoring undergraduates. That is a testament to his talent.

He lived alone in a little house on Athens Street just outside of Harvard Square.

I was terrified when I was admitted as a transfer student to Harvard. The summer before my first classes, I had seen *Hogan's Goat* on TV. It was great. I couldn't get enough of it.

I was terrified of the place but I was a determined starstruck groupie with a plan.

As soon as I got my student ID, I went to Nick at Brattle Florist in Harvard Square. Nick was a proprietor and a friend. I had started buying corsages from him in high school, and I loved just going into his shop to talk to him.

I had decided to buy flowers and knock on Professor Alfred's door to tell him the truth about being a starstruck groupie who just wanted to meet him.

Nick told me that Professor Alfred came in regularly, so he knew his favorite fresh flowers.

I took my bouquet early in the afternoon to Professor Alfred's little house. I carefully ascended the three steps and almost knocked on his door, but I lost my nerve. I made two more passes before I finally knocked on the door and waited.

When he answered, I immediately straight-armed my flowers at him as I stood on the top step and I told him I was a transfer student who knew no one but I was a big fan of his and then I turned to go. He thanked me and to my surprise he said, "Come in. I'm making tea."

I entered his little living room and sat in one of the wing chairs next to a little fireplace with a small clock on the mantle.

Professor Alfred returned with the flowers in a vase and a pot of tea with cups. He settled in and started to ask me questions. I was caught completely off guard. I talked too much about myself because I was nervous. But finally, I had the sense to ask him questions about the play as I kept an eye on the little clock on the mantle. I did not want to outstay my welcome, but I didn't want to leave.

After almost 25 minutes, I stood up and apologized for staying so long, and Professor Alford asked me, "Do you have a Tutor?" I didn't know what a Tutor was so I was sure I could confidently tell him, "No, I don't." He promptly replied, "I can be your Tutor." I promptly accepted, even though I had no idea what that meant.

That night, I went to my first dinner at Kirkland House, my new dorm along the river. I had been assigned a room and I told the three or four boys who randomly settled their trays at my table that I was a transfer student and I wondered if they knew what a Tutor was. I was told it was like a graduate student who was sort of an academic big brother. I told them I had randomly met Professor Alfred that afternoon and he had offered to be my Tutor.

My dinner companions were shocked. "You're kidding! Alfred is your Tutor?" The next day, I rented a room on Putnam Avenue and never stopped studying for fear I would flunk out.

I was convinced that once my fellow classmates at Harvard discovered how stupid I was, it would be the rage of the campus and I would be pointed out continuously, so I never moved into Kirkland house.

For two years, once a week at 8:30 a.m., I met Professor Alfred and we studied poetry together. At the end of each meeting he would ask, "What do you want to learn next week?" There were no limits. We talked about Greek metrics and rhymes in English and non-English in translation, and poetry all the way back through Beowulf.

In the spring, we would set up two chairs in his little backyard and he would feed the squirrels by hand as we talked. Quite unconsciously, he became my poetic surrogate father. In short, I fell in love with the man, the devout Catholic, the humanitarian and the poet.

He would at times quote from memory poems he liked. One time, he quoted: "There is in God (some say) A deep, but dazzling darkness…"

It was by Henry Vaughan (1621–1695), but I didn't take in the rest of it. His recitation had stopped me in my tracks because of the way he delivered it. He measured out the rhythm in the air and there was an intensity in the way he looked at me that made me lose my concentration.

Although Professor Alfred was in late middle age, he loved life, and I loved that he rose to almost any occasion.

One morning as I entered, Robert Lowell, the famous poet, was leaving. Professor Alfred explained, "Cal wanted to go see the *artistes* last night." They had gone down to the "combat zone" in Boston because Lowell, the old Brahman, very much out of character, wanted to see the strippers at work.

One morning as I entered, Faye Dunaway, the star of *Hogan's Goat*, and Peter Wolf, the lead singer for The J. Geils Band, were on the couch in the living room. The two had obviously been on a very creative overnighter, and Alfred had sat up with them because they were friends.

I graduated with honors in 1973, and when I would visit Boston or Cambridge I'd visit Nick to pick up flowers and knock on Alfred's door. If he was in we would always talk.

It was always professor/student but it was always friend to friend. The phone would ring occasionally, and he would smile and say, "They will call back I am certain," and we would talk some more. The friendship ripened and grew stronger over time.

In June of 1999, I traveled up to Cambridge and ambled into the Brattle Street Florist, found Nick and requested my customary bouquet of flowers. Nick looked up from the flowers he was arranging for a customer. He dried his hands as he stopped his work to talk to me. He faced me, paused, and said, "He died last month. He's up in the Harvard lot in Mt. Auburn Cemetery."

I read in *The Crimson* that the Brattle Florist would be closing.

Nick had died but I stopped there when I was in Cambridge and got flowers. I took them to Mt Auburn and found Alfred's grave below the tower, up the hill.

The gravestone reads:

"There is in God (some say)
A deep but dazzling darkness –
O for that night! where I in him
Might live invisible and dim."

I had missed those last two lines when he'd read them, which defined him perfectly.

There was no one around, so I spent a lot of time with him, and when I got up, my knees were wet from the ground. I think I loved him more then than I ever had before.

Photo: Archives and Special Collections, Vassar College Library

A Little Pat on the Back from a Long Time Ago

I previously wrote about Professor William Alfred, my Tutor in college, and how my affection has grown for him. Today, I will remember the other mentor for whom I have a continued and growing affection.

Elizabeth Bishop (1911–1979) was, and still is, a very respected poet of the late 20th Century. She lived a hard life filled with loss and loneliness. She was raised and passed around by her maternal grandparents and relatives after her father died when she was a year old and her mother was placed in a mental hospital.

After she got into and graduated from Vassar, because she had no traditional family to surround her, she found comfort in travel. In late midlife, after her partner with whom she lived in Brazil for years died, she was alone again. Robert Lowell convinced Harvard to offer her a chance to teach there.

In order to get into her class in the fall of 1972, I had to submit an essay on the Wallace Stevens poem "The Emperor of Ice Cream."

It starts:

Call the roller of big cigars,
The muscular one, and bid him whip
In kitchen cups concupiscent curds.

It is a difficult poem. It is like a description of a carnival with its cigar rollers and ice cream makers, but it is about the preparations for a Cuban funeral. It is a celebration of life, not a celebration of the dead person. The end of the first stanza reads:

Let be be finale of seem.
The only emperor is the emperor of ice-cream.

From my first reading it struck me personally as being so godless and lonely. It ends with this:

If her horny feet protrude, they come
To show how cold she is, and dumb.
Let the lamp affix its beam.
The only emperor is the emperor of ice-cream.

Years later, I found in her letters her description of how she had decided to choose that poem for the competition.

She was walking alone past Brigham's Ice Cream in Harvard Square toward Kirkland House, where she would make copies of the poem she had chosen for the competition and leave it with Alice Methfessel, a staff person there, to hand out to the competitors.

Alice would, a few years later, become the executor of Bishop's estate.

It was a small class limited to around 10 to 12 people. She required that each student memorize 15 lines of two 20th Century poets for each class. She was insistent. When she pointed at us in class, we had to recite our chosen poems.

She told us it was a way to bring a poem alive again. When it was recited in a different environment it will be different than reading it from a book again and again. It was like a friendship you could carry with you.

Bishop did not appreciate self-centered over-egoed undergraduates. I was a little older myself. From the beginning, I believed I felt her loneliness and I imagined she felt mine, but I wrote it off as my imagination.

I worked very hard in Bishop's class and she saw the depth of my interest and commitment. I didn't speak up much but I was always prepared for class. I never made intentional eye contact but I found that midway through the term she smiled after I had participated, and by the end of the year we would even talk briefly as we were leaving class to reenter the Square.

We talked about things rather than poems when we chatted. This was a time when confessional poetry was on the rise and people wrote very personally about their families and themselves extensively, but Bishop by nature was reserved and private. She wrote about things that were indirect, but they were very moving and profoundly personal.

No one believes me now, but I misread the instructions for the first hour of the three-hour blue book final exam. The instruction required that we were to write out verbatim half of all those poems that we had memorized. I wrote out all of them.

I got an A from her, and Professor Alfred was pleased because she had a reputation for being a hard grader.

I asked her to write a recommendation when I applied to law school. She agreed, but I was surprised to almost sense she thought my choice was a little misguided given my obvious love of the arts. I don't think she thought too highly of lawyers.

Years later, well after she had died, I was surprised to learn her recommendations could still be found at Kirkland House, so I asked to see hers of me. I proudly made a copy and, when I read it, I discovered something.

She wrote a short but glowing recommendation, but she concluded:

"... but I feel he has great abilities, and possibly talents, he is not aware of himself... Mr. Bowie has worked very hard and has a very original cast of mind. I recommend him highly."

What an odd and gratuitous comment for a law school recommendation, I thought. Did she know someday I would find it?

And then I smiled as if she had touched my hand.

She had cared about me. And as I stood there rereading my Xerox copy, I felt affirmed and supported to continue on this, my late life journey. She had noticed me.

The Older You Get the Shorter Your Stories Should Be

Elizabeth Bishop, Cemeteries, and Contrast as Creativity

I'm extremely fortunate to have had a class with Elizabeth Bishop, who was one of our great, late 20th Century poets. She taught us that any two poems, no matter where they are from, when placed side-by-side will cause an unintended contrast that will illuminate both.

Once grasped, this is an eye-opening idea with endless potentiality for creative thought.

I grew up between two schools, two cemeteries, and Harvard Square. The Cambridge cemetery was relatively flat, had few trees, was wide open, and pretty much existed to hold the military dead of foreign wars and the citizens of that city.

In contrast, behind the impenetrable black iron fence and gate of Mount Auburn Cemetery, spread a small and elite universe of acres of hills and valleys with shaded walkways and still ponds, as an arboretum of carefully preserved trees and as an aviary for local and migrating birds. These two cemeteries existed side by side divided only by a single two-lane road.

As children, we would freely ride our bikes among the military dead in the Cambridge cemetery, but we were strictly prohibited from even entering Mount Auburn. It wasn't a place designed for us.

However, when the gates were open, adults were permitted to walk among the graves and in its verdant splendor. Mount Auburn rested like a shared understanding of what a patrician heaven might be, while the Cambridge Cemetery was a plebeian limbo.

When I visited after last Memorial Day, the Cambridge cemetery had rows and rows of flags. One at each grave. No one was there except a lone bagpiper striding along one of the empty roads. Unexpectedly, I could find only one flag in all of Mount Auburn, and it was guarded by a wild turkey that had become domesticated by the place. There was a quiet urgency as groups of horticulturalists or birdwatchers clustered and whispered observations to each other.

Miss Bishop, as she called herself, was right. The accident of the unintended contrasts caused by my time and location that day opened up worlds for me about the two cemeteries, about the living generation and the predeceased, as I walked between the four.

Life After Nitrogen Narcosis?

In our class, the poet Elizabeth Bishop would teach poetry by taking any two poems and placing them side by side to see how they "illuminated each other" by comparison and contrast.

It was an exercise in both observation and communication, but it also offered that fresh perspective on what was set in stone and had been taken for granted.

The more extreme the comparison and contrast the more it reawakens: A ripe apple and a red sports car? What makes them red? What makes them different? What makes them go? DNA and water versus oil and a gas engine?

How about like "politics" and "scuba diving"?

Let's try it.

Well first, in contrast, they encompass two different worlds. One above water and one below. However, people have learned to communicate in both worlds, particularly in life-threatening situations.

How is that communication the same and different, and how can it offer a fresh perspective?

Through communication in politics, Donald Trump raised a quarter of a billion dollars ($250,000,000.00) from small dollar contributions from his supporters to "stop the steal," despite overwhelming evidence that nothing got stolen. Furthermore, he has convinced his supporters not to watch the January 6th Committee hearings where this was revealed and validated.

So you can't use Twitter underwater.

But in scuba diving you have hand signals, which is a little more primitive but just as effective for short urgent messages.

All diving is done in at least pairs, with each diver responsible for his or her buddy. If you go too deep and become a victim of nitrogen narcosis — which is the song of angels calling you to come deeper to your death. Your buddy should grab your fin and signal with a hand gesture indicating the cutting of one's throat, then point to the surface. It's life or death.

During one dive in the outer islands of the Caribbean, I was randomly paired with two Midwestern middle-aged men who already were friends.

We agreed to go down to about 90 feet and swim in formation, like airplanes, to cruise along the deep edge of a cliff overhang and be each other's eyes and ears.

One of my new buddies, our wing man at the time, banged his knife on his tank to get our attention, made eye contact, and excitedly pointed straight down. He spread his arms way out wide, gave the finger to us, and then put his right hand on his head at a 90-degree angle as if it was splitting his head in half down the middle with an ax. The other two of us got it and looked down into the dark for a "Big Fucking Shark!"

Later that afternoon, sitting side by side with me at the bar, my two Midwestern buddies good-naturedly unloaded all the liberal Democrat jokes they had in rapid fire in my direction, and with mock astonishment I countered them with my defenses and went on the attack.

Quite naturally we had come to trust each other with our lives underwater, using sign language that we made up as we went along. We were friends.

I would love to meet them again and learn from them again and laugh. I want to sit on that barstool, turn to look at them and, with a perfectly timed pause, stop deadpan and say: "TRUMP???" And then spread my arms out wide, give them the finger and put my right hand on my head at a right angle as if it was splitting my head down the middle with an ax. I'd love to have them laugh at that, for us to laugh together.

I want to laugh with my Republican friends again and have us trust each other again with our lives.

It beats drowning in an angel's call.

Chum in the Water

This is the story behind one of the sonnets in my book, *An Accidental Diary*.

Sometimes you have to be far above a mistake before you acknowledge that you made it. In my case, it was flying from Belize and looking out the window more than 25 years ago.

The Blue Hole of Belize is a prehistoric giant crater that is over 400 feet deep and 43 miles out to sea from Belize City. From Ambergris Caye, an offshore island east of Belize City, it's about a two-and-a-half hour rough ride in a small Boston Whaler, depending on the weather.

The Blue Hole was made famous by Jacques Cousteau in 1971 when he brought his ship The Calypso to the Blue Hole to chart its depth and explore its history.

Almost 30 years later, in the summer of 1997, an expedition of cave divers went in to document its underwater stalactite caves and search for its bottom depths.

Around this time, I went with several expert divers. We found it was pretty much empty of sea creatures and very cold as you descended ever deeper into it. We went down 150 feet to the nitrogen limits for two minutes. Our flashlight beams dimmed into the nothingness in that dark. If you looked up, far above us, the sky was like a distant open manhole cover and was our only meaningful light.

After listening in the silence to our breathing for the two minutes, we ascended slowly with our bubbles to avoid nitrogen build up in our blood stream. It was very dark, cold, claustrophobic, and dangerous. Other divers had reported the same thing. After that dive I decided: "Well, been there, done that; never again."

A few years later, when I was again in Belize to dive the outer islands, two Ambergris Caye teenage brothers with a little Boston Whaler bet me a case of beer one night in a beachfront bar that if I went with them the following morning, it would be the most amazing dive I'd ever done. I refused and refused until I took the bet. This was a very stupid thing for me to have done.

In December 2018, 20 years later, two small submarines were sent to map the Blue Hole's interior. At the bottom they discovered the bodies of two of the three divers who had gone missing while diving there over the years.

The Blue Hole in Belize

Was I the fool of this sinkhole of the sea
Or a pupil in this aqua ocean?
As I fly home it looks back at me
Without memory or emotion.

Three days ago, while taunting me, Miguel
Said: "You've dived it but not with me before.
I dive it deep. I dive it right to hell."
He took my money but wouldn't tell me more.

Off the boat, with Miguel still behind,
We checked our gear and descended into cold,
Deeper, darker, to fear of a different kind:
Sharks. Hundreds of them. Darting from the shadows.

At the boat Miguel offered a helping hand,
Laughing." You understand? We chummed it man."

The Older You Get the Shorter Your Stories Should Be

Townie in Cambridge

Photo: Massachusetts Office of Travel & Tourism; CC BY-ND 2.0

From Before the Beginning

The great thing about being a geezer is there are moments when you actually existed before history.

Last weekend, Head of the Charles, the world's largest two-day regatta, with 11,000 American and international athletes in over 1,900 boats competing in 61 events, was held on a three-mile course (4,800 meters) on the Charles River between Boston and Cambridge, Massachusetts.

On that beautiful fall weekend, more than 225,000 people gathered to watch, either on the banks of a clean water river or shoulder to shoulder on both sides of the six bridges under which the crews travel. The race has increased in participants and prestige since its beginnings in 1965.

Now I know what you're thinking. I am going to claim credit for something. I'm probably going to brag that I was there at the beginning or something like that but I'm not.

I was there before the beginning!

I was there back when nobody dared gather on the banks or bridges because they might fall in. Back when The Standells recorded "Love That Dirty Water (down by the river Charles)" in a pop hit in the '60s. Back when I had decided I liked girls but I really hated school and was discouraged about myself and I was trying out for crew to row on a polluted river.

High School Crew

In the early spring, when I turned fifteen,
My choices were baseball, tennis or crew.
Between Boston and Cambridge I had seen
Rhythmic oars of singles, eights, fours and twos

Beneath the bridges of the Charles River.
I was appointed stroke. I paced the boat.
Like a surgeon's stitch our sharp blades suture
The shell's trailing razor cut as each stroke

Drives us through the smooth and glassy water
And leaves no scar. The coxswain pounds out,
On the gunnels, the rhythm of my order.
Tin cans and prophylactics float past the boat.

Our smooth and perfect rhythmic mantra broke
Beneath the bridges, into echoes: "Stroke. Stroke."

I like these little prehistory events. They show me if I start from before the beginning, rather than in the midst of some turmoil, I can see how much has changed for the better.

The Older You Get the Shorter Your Stories Should Be

Photo: David Ohmer; CC BY-ND 2.0

A Halloween Ghost Story

Previously, I wrote about this year's Head of the Charles Regatta, and the beautiful clean water of the Charles River. This was in contrast to years ago when I was in ninth grade and the river was so dirty, we rowed past floating prophylactics and tin cans and even a floating pillow that turned over and was a dead body — later identified as Eno English.

It didn't occur to me until last week, but I think I know where Eno might have come from.

I grew up in a little neighborhood called Coolidge Hill near the boat house and dock where Eno was found floating in the Charles. Coolidge Hill is located in between the Cambridge and Mount Auburn cemeteries and the little school I attended.

Mount Auburn cemetery was created in 1831 to house the Cambridge aristocracy on 170 acres of high rolling land with little walks along majestic ponds surrounded by an impenetrably high black iron fence.

Mount Auburn Cemetery allowed no bikes or unsupervised children. I got my first bike, a fat wheeler, in middle school. I tried but could not get past the gate house on my bike, but I decided I would not be denied.

With my first bike I became an explorer. Like Columbus was

determined to find the Orient, I decided I had to find a way into Mount Auburn Cemetery. I decided I would explore what I guessed might be the unguarded back fence near the Charles River.

Late one afternoon I left school and took my bike down past the boat house and proceeded upriver along the deserted overgrown roadless riverbank for a quarter mile or so to find, much to my satisfaction, that there was some fence on the western border of the cemetery that had fallen with the eroding high bank. It must have given way with the rains and snow over the years and had slipped down onto a very small muddy plateau next to the Charles.

When I stopped to look I saw, to my surprise, a little path leading down to the river to the left, and several loose rolls of toilet paper hanging off a low bush. To my right I saw two small shacks that had been pulled together and hidden under several small scrub trees and underbrush up closer to the cemetery and the broken fence.

It must have been late fall, after Halloween I think, because it was getting dark early and it was a school night. I concluded that hobos must've lived here in the summer and had left because the weather was getting cold. There was no evidence of smoking fires or habitation.

As I laid down my bike and worked my way into the underbrush, I saw there were no windows in the two shacks and the doors had been left open. As I approached one shack, I stepped on several bones that looked like they had been brought down with the erosion of the cemetery. I remember them as spongy, but I pushed on through the undergrowth because I could see through the open door what appeared to be girly magazines.

This lured me on because my only other alternative had been at the doctor's office when I had to pretend to be interested in National Geographic. I pushed closer and closer to the open door.

The magazines were scattered all over the dirt floor and there was a pile of blankets over to the right. I carefully moved into the shack and knelt down to the magazines. The sun was going down. It was getting cold. I was alone. I had to get home but as long as there was light, I was going to see what this bounty held.

As I picked up one of the water-soaked magazines I was startled by an abrupt movement under the pile of blankets and a face stared back at me.

I bolted for the door and ran for my life to my bicycle. The man stood, reached for me and yelled. I ran as fast as I could, mounted my bike and peddled furiously until I could no longer hear his breathing.

The newspapers postured that Eno must've fallen into the river because his fly was open when he was fished out of the water.

That was almost 60 years ago.

My little bike ride along the Charles is paved now as Greenough Boulevard. It travels along the river's edge and into new parking lots and developments along Arsenal Avenue and Watertown.

As far as I can tell there is no record of Eno English other than in my memory. He is a ghost that lives in my imagination and shelters in my brain and only came out with a random recollection a few days before Halloween.

Sort of spooky. Time for Eno to disappear again.

How the Hell Did You Get into They'a?

Perhaps it was always just a place in time but, for me, it was the reality of my youth. Its boundaries were Harvard Square to the east, my home on Coolidge Hill with Mount Auburn Cemetery and Cambridge Cemetery to the north, two schools — Shady Hill and Browne & Nichols — to the west, and the Charles River to my south.

But all of this was lived in the shadow of Harvard University during the Kennedy years and later the Vietnam War.

I was all in. I was a townie from birth. The athletes on the football and hockey teams were my rock stars, and the professors would take time off from the university to advise United States presidents who were graduates.

If you were fortunate to be admitted, I believed you were blessed for life and, starting with your freshman year, you would be offered an education unequaled anywhere else in the world.

It took me several expulsions, numerous worthless summer schools with worthless speed reading classes if you were a dyslexic, a condition that, for me, went undiagnosed for years. All in all, it took six years but I finally got through high school.

Anyway, I was determined to get into Harvard.

The Cambridge School of Weston, a progressive school in the suburbs of Boston, took me in but required that I repeat 11th grade and start working with Mr. Johnson, a trained reading teacher, who convinced me to finally take an IQ test and start fresh with the alphabet. When I asked, he smiled and he told me, "Yes, you can go to college."

I immediately packed up my report cards and went to The Harvard admissions office, where I announced that my problems would soon be solved and I would be going to Harvard.

I met with one of the admissions officers, Deke Smith, who went over my report cards, then looked up at me inquisitively and said, "You have never gotten anything better than a C+." I was ready for him, and responded, "Well, they take 20 points off for spelling."

He gently said that I would have to be president of my school, president of the literary magazine, as well as president of the New England Student Government Association, which encompasses all New England prep schools and their student governments. In hindsight, I'm pretty sure I was being offered the door, but I didn't know that.

My senior year I went back to Mr. Smith and informed him that I had accomplished those three goals, and he looked at me sort of long and hard and apologized. "I did not mean to lead you on, but all we do here is read books and write papers. I don't think you could survive."

I applied anyway and was rejected.

I went off to a wonderful school in Ohio, left the campus dorms, rented an apartment in the town and went underground. In September of 1970, I was in a high-speed motorcycle crash, which killed the driver, my friend. I spent the next several months hanging from the ceiling in a pelvic sling in multiple hospitals until I ended up back in Boston and Cambridge, where I started to move again in wheelchairs and on crutches.

I had a moment of genius.

I went back to Mr. Smith at the admissions office and told him that I would not be able to go back to school that spring and hoped he would let me be a "special student" at Harvard so I could take one class and get credit for it when I returned to Ohio the next year.

He was shocked to see me again but remembered me. He reiterated that I might survive with one class because, as he had said, "All we do here is read books and write papers."

I got my student ID and realized I was inside the walls and I was living my plan.

I signed up for five classes, not just one, and told my mother that I would do all the research because I had nothing better to do than go to the library on crutches, but I asked her would she type my papers to avoid the spelling issues. She laughed and agreed and I went to work.

I did nothing but work and sleep and go to class and work for that entire spring semester. My one fear was the Blue Book hourly exams where I would have to write out my answers and reveal my spelling issues. I expected I would lose 20 points for spelling. When I got the Blue Book back, there were red marks all the way through it. But about two-thirds of the way in they stopped, and at the very end, in red pen, was, "You know your stuff but your spelling is atrocious. A-."

I didn't stop celebrating for a week.

After I got my report card, I went back to Mr. Smith and showed him I had gotten all A's and B's except for one C+, which then put me at least in the middle of the class.

He looked like a guy who just had his pants pulled down. I told him that I would be applying as a transfer student for admission the next year, then smiled at him and left.

He was defenseless.

Several months later, I got the fat envelope. I proudly walked into my parents' bedroom as my father was reading in the late afternoon on the bed, and I told him I just got into Harvard. He smiled and offered congratulations then went back to reading. It was not his ambition, it was mine. I went to the kitchen to tell my mother and we, in fact, celebrated.

In 1973, I graduated with honors. Fifty years later at our 50th reunion, I met classmates who I had never met before and, only then, felt that I finally fit in, even though I did not qualify for admission. I thought I had justified my acceptance and graduation because I had loved that education so much!

That school gave me a chance that others wouldn't. That school looked deeper into me than all the other schools, other than the Cambridge School of Weston, ever had. I felt for the first time I was one of them and worthy to be one of their classmates.

I live in Maryland now, as I have for years, but I really am very much still that Cambridge townie. Only weeks ago, when we were at Oriole spring training together, my son looked at me very seriously and asked, "Are you actually a closet Red Sox fan?"

The Older You Get the Shorter Your Stories Should Be

Photo: Massachusets Office of Travel and Tourism; CC BY-ND 2.0

There Is Something Wonderful About Random Spontaneity!

I am learning to trust and believe in random spontaneity!

Although I have been blessed with many friends, since I have committed to writing full time, I have been painfully aware that I have few friends who are poets with whom I could converse.

The stars aligned perfectly last week when something wonderful happened. And then things just kept getting randomly better and better...

I had just gotten five copies of the final draft of my first book of poems, *An Accidental Diary*, from Kerry Sharda, my wonderful book designer. All of a sudden, the prospect of publishing became very real for me. So last weekend I took action.

I booked an impromptu trip to Boston to get advice on the book from a friend and two professors I adore about publishing this first book of poems. I then quite unexpectedly got to meet two poets I had previously never met but greatly admire.

I also had been waiting throughout the pandemic to congratulate Belinda Rathbone on her new book, *George Rickey: A Life in Balance*, about the life and work of the famous kinetic sculptor.

I called Belinda hoping to meet her and get her advice but she told me that she was on her way to Scotland. After I told her about my mission, she told me that I should meet Lloyd Schwartz and Gail Mazur, both frequently published and very well-respected poets, both of whom were her friends.

I jumped at this unexpected opportunity. How could this be getting better and better? I had their books and decided to bring along the most recent books of new and selected work, *Who's on First?* by Schwartz and *Land's End* by Mazur, in the hope I could get them autographed.

We agreed to meet at Harvest, a restaurant in Harvard Square. I decided to be early but recognized Lloyd from his book cover photographs as he entered the restaurant and said, "I figured that must've been you because you were carrying all those books."

Shortly after we were seated, Gail joined us and we talked for over two-and-a-half hours. We had an amazing link: We had all known the poet Elizabeth Bishop. I had only been her student once but they knew her well and Lloyd had written his PhD thesis on her and was a scholar of her works.

In addition, during our conversation I revealed that Robert Pinsky's translation of Dante's *Inferno* was a favorite of mine and Gail and Lloyd both told me they knew him and that Gail's late husband had done the remarkable artwork for that book.

After the lunch crowd had emptied out and we finally left, Gail offered to walk over to The Charles Hotel to show me some of her husband's works that were prominently on display as complete panels on the walls. They were as amazing as the illustrations for Pinsky's *Inferno*.

This was a remarkable weekend for me because though I love my friends I have painfully few friends who are poets.

To be surrounded by these wonderful creators as we freely talked about overlapping themes was overwhelming for me. The two were longtime friends and both agreed that creativity requires interchange and friendship to nurture artistic endeavor.

We agreed to meet again when I next came to Boston. I felt welcome and included and re-dedicated to this, my new and ever exciting profession.

It was all a spontaneous accident, which I come to believe more and more is what art and life is.

I have so much more to do.

Photo: Jon Chase/Harvard University. Poems reprinted by permission, © 2019, 2020, 2023.

Don't Settle for a Low Paying Job, Be a Poet Laureate!

If you loved your education or even if you didn't, but love the people, the culture — and you are pretty certain you should have never been admitted — you are a born Poet Laureate.

If you are worried about qualifications, no license is required. And what is really great is that there are endless jobs available because in most institutions this job has not even been created — so you can fill it by volunteering and hold it endlessly as long as you are keeping the alumni laughing.

And if you are worried about keeping your integrity this is absolutely the job for you! You can test this:

Call a restaurant and tell them you are a Poet Laureate. You will get a table next to the kitchen. You can insist on no favoritism and be certain that your request will be honored.

And it is not "a low paying job"! It is a *no* paying job, so you pay no taxes! And there are other hidden benefits:

I have found that as long as I have been a Poet Laureate they have not revoked my degree. In my case, that's important.

I have been the Poet Laureate of the Harvard Alumni Association for over ten years. The job requires that I present my "ode" at the Annual

Spring Meetings of the Alumni Association. In 2019, I celebrated *Harvard Magazine* and my former father-in-law, both of whom I love:

For Harvard Magazine
(Portrait of Gentleman Jim)

Whenever I became too confident
Of my perfect Harvard education
My ex-father-in-law, concomitant,
Was there to deliver expiation.
His timing was perfect. He'd watch and wait.
He'd set me up and then he'd set me straight.

Let me describe this kind and gentle man:
In profile he was blessed with a perfect
Semi-circular belly and no can.
Perfect as a backlit window silhouette:
A photo I still love and regret.
A photo my ex-wife wouldn't forget.

A small piece of a small, but sad divorce.
He has 'passed on' but I miss the man.
Comfortable with himself. Steady. On course.
Leaning back with a scotch glass in his hand,
"I sell seeds and satisfy farmers' needs,
Go to church, plant the garden, pull the weeds."

Every Easter the two of us would go
Outside to smoke illegal Cuban cigars.
He'd get me to tell him what he should know.
He'd always wait until I'd gone too far.
He'd lean back: "Ahh, hoist by your own petard?"
Flick off his ash and say "Harvard-smavard."

They're all gone now, his wife, mine and him.
But still up until the very end
I would package and carry up to him
All my old Harvard Magazines and then
He always put them there in the same place,
Next to the kindling and fireplace.

I drove up a month or so before he died.
He so deeply missed his loving wife.
The reconciliations I had tried
Had failed. Love was leaking out of his life.
The door unlocked, sleeping in his chair
With a Harvard Magazine spread out there

Heaving on his perfect snoring belly,
What a perfect find was all of this?
There was food in the ice box from the deli.
I found whiskey and two glasses. I kissed
Him and asked "What's this you're reading you fool?"
With a cagey smile: "It ain't that bad a school."

(There's video here: robertbowiejr.com/haa-harvard-magazine.
For the last few years, for different reasons, my ode has been videoed
You can find more videos at robertbowiejr.com/youtube.)

During the pandemic, I celebrated Harvard's amazing football history
and bemoaned the cancellation of our graduation and my 50th reunion:

Rose Bowl
(Our Virtual Graduation)

"A Spirit moved. John Harvard walked the Yard.
The books stood open and the gates unbarred."
I quote Seamus Heaney. Cause he's a real Rock Star.
I'm not, so imagine the gates are not unbarred...
Because I'm quarantined and locked out of Harvard Yard
With my ode to football history and our student stars!

But first, since Harvard must be first, because God has made it so —
Harvard invented football! Here's how that story goes:
Back in 1869, Rutgers and Princeton
Claimed they played no passing, carrying and no run,
No pads, no helmets, wrong ball, not even blockers!
They claimed they played the first football game, but that was soccer!

Thank "heaven" five years thereafter, Harvard played McGill
In an international collegiate game of skill.
Thank "heaven" Harvard's rules were used, and they came to be,
To replace the rules for kickball in backwoods New Jersey.
Harvard is "veritas!" So, what's the mystery?
First game? Right rules! God knows who rewrote that history!

And then "a spirit moved" the Class of '79.
In 1903 they built it, ahead of its time...
In mid-November, just one month before man could fly...
An above ground bomb shelter with a fifty-yard line...
If you think that stadium money went down the drain
Consider, a century ago, we won the Rose Bowl game

And seven national championships were also won,
With six big Rhodes Scholars (each maybe a tenth of a ton)
And seventeen conference titles and we're not even done
Because it looks like Coach Murphy is still having tons of fun.
Forty-two varsity sports. The most in Division One.
Our Scholar Athletes test real well and they also can chew gum!

Yes, it's sad for all of us! Quarantined from the Yard,
Exiled from graduation. Alums is what we are!
So, let's summon Seamus Heaney. He is our trusted bard,
To turn our prayers to poetry and realign our stars:
Let's pray soon a spirit moves and John Harvard will walk the Yard
And the books will reopen and soon, for all of us, the gates can be unbarred.

The 50th Reunion of the Class of 1973
(and a Tip of the Hat to the Class of 2023)

So is this where sex, drugs, and rock 'n' roll ends?
With grandchildren, prostate problems and Depends?
Not for the class of 1973
On this, our 50th anniversary!
We're the Alums that never stopped having fun...
For us our college years were just a dry run!

So why try to remember what I've forgot?
Maybe it's a little. Maybe it's a lot.
Who cares? Fifty years of paranoia
Now pot's legal'n, some say, even good for ya.
Forget that thought that we are all old relics.
Now shrinks treat patients with our psychedelics.

Memory and "smarts" never go hand in glove.
I've no memory of what my major was.
Who cares, long as they don't take my diploma back
If my "memory lane" is a cul-de-sac!
I do still remember my graduation!
That 50th, class of '23, had some fun!

I'll tell you the whole truth. I'll tell you no lie.
Wasn't exactly "Fast Times at Ridgemont High."
Them dancing to James Brown and breaking a sweat.
Man, that is one thing I really regret.
Yes, we lived through some stuff you just can't forget:
Watergate, Berlin Wall, and the Chia Pet.

But wait! Just stop and wait. I wonder what we
Look like to the grads of 2023?
They have evolved so much! They're truly phenoms.
They're so advanced I check for hair on my palms.
I still type with both hands and I feel real dumb.
Darwin was right. Now they can type with their thumbs.

Oh, but we've got wisdom in the class of '73!
First, you must accept Harvard's study on longevity.
It is not your new Harvard degree or your new PhD.
Joy comes from your classmates, and your friends and your family.
Second, the older you get the shorter your stories should be.
And last, "Peace 'n Love!" from the great class of '73.

In truth, this is not just a labor of love. It is more than that. I owe this school more than I can ever pay back. For me, it is my foolish way to say thank you — worth doing for that alone. If your institution does not have a Poet Laureate, volunteer. You can make a fool of yourself and open doors for others to be free to do the same.

A Walk-Off Ninth-Inning Home Run

As a young boy, I lived in the sports pages and played on sandlot baseball diamonds after school. I dreamed about the big leagues. My dreams and my future were one.

As a young man, things became a little more complicated.

I couldn't really hit a curve ball and I started noticing that the second question that people asked grown-ups after their name was "What do you do?"

Businessman? Doctor? Lawyer? With high school, a wider and more terrifying world was opening up.

I stumbled on T.S. Eliot and his poem, "The Love Song of J. Alfred Prufrock," in which he wrote about the early 20th century. It is set in Boston's Beacon Hill.

It seduced me from my fading childhood into my predestined future with its opening lines:

Let us go then, you and I,
When the evening is spread out against the sky
Like a patient etherized upon a table;

Ezra Pound pronounced this poem as "modern" — part of the dark reality of the new century and its new poetry. And so it was for me, standing there, in the Grolier Poetry Book Shop with J. Alfred Prufrock in my hand, a freshly minted teenage groupie at a one-room bookstore with towering bookcases.

Grolier was intimidating, but it held a world of new alternative heroes as I was losing my childhood and falling into the shadows of some job that would define me when asked "What do you do?"

How did this happen?

Posted on the front door of Grolier Poetry Book Shop was a blunt sign: "No Law. No History. No Economics. No Biology. No Physics. No Chemistry. Only Poetry!"

Gordon Cairnie, one of the founders, would sit on an old couch and hold court with published poets who were different in every way than the people I knew.

He waited for some unsuspecting student to walk in and ask if the store sold law books or the like.

Gordon would unload on the innocent walk-in and turn all the heads of the browsing readers when at the top of his voice he would answer, "No! But what difference does it make to you because you can't even read the sign!"

Everyone would laugh in this freshly reconsecrated space and the young student was sure never to return.

The point of entry to this new world was the "dare to be different" commitment to admit out loud that you were a poet and a believer, not a tourist.

I was way too shy.

This was a lot different than sandlot baseball, but within it there was still room to dream.

Over the years, the Grolier had become a focus of poetic activity in the Cambridge area, itself a magnet for American poets because of the influence of Harvard University. Poets such as John Ashbery, Robert Bly,

Robert Creeley, Donald Hall, and Frank O'Hara were regulars at the store during their time as undergraduates at Harvard. The poet Conrad Aiken lived upstairs from the store in its early days.

Numerous other poets and writers are noted as "friends of the Grolier," including Russell Banks, Frank Bidart, William Corbett, E. E. Cummings, T. S. Eliot, Lawrence Ferlinghetti, David Ferry, Allen Ginsberg, Denise Levertov, Marianne Moore, Charles Olson, Robert Pinsky, Adrienne Rich, Ruth Stone, James Tate and Franz Wright, to name just a few.

The bookstore claims to be the oldest continuous bookshop devoted solely to the sale of poetry and poetry criticism.

In September of 2022, it will be 95 years old.

I was committed to keeping up with the rest, going to law school and succeeding — and I did. But I couldn't forget the voices at Grolier and my prior fear of admitting out loud I wanted to be a poet.

When my travels would lead me to Boston, I would always go back to make sure it was still there. I would always buy a book or two to justify my visit and my love of lounging there for a while.

Last Saturday, I was in Cambridge. I brought two copies of my first book of poems, An Accidental Diary, to give to friends I planned to see.

That morning in the hotel room, an idea hit me. I looked up the Grolier Poetry Bookstore and, before I let better judgment kick in, I called and asked for the proprietor, James Fraser.

I told him I had two copies of a book, explaining one poem was runner up for the Robert Frost Foundation Poetry Award and another had been chosen for an upcoming anthology in Baltimore. I asked him if he would consider putting them up for sale on the shelves.

I told James I had been going into the bookstore for over 50 years and had studied with Professor William Alfred and Elizabeth Bishop whose books were on the shelves and pictures on the walls.

He invited me to drop by. I immediately walked my two books over and told him more of my story. I encouraged him to read "Summer Thunderstorms" and "The Facts of Life" to show the range of the work.

He leafed through the book as we continue to talk. There were a few people browsing as there always are and I took a moment to take a deep breath and just be surrounded by the place.

James looked up and smiled. He took both books out of my hand, looked up at me again, took one for the shelf and then put one book prominently in the front window.

Things this wonderful don't really happen in real life but sometimes they do.

When I walked back to the hotel empty-handed looking down at the pavement with a stupid grin on my face, I felt like I had circled the bases on the sandlot!

I had always dreamed about the big leagues. But after a very long time my dreams and my future were again one.

The Older You Get the Shorter Your Stories Should Be

It Can't Happen Here

"It Can't Happen Here"

"It can't happen here." — Frank Zappa

Since recorded history, our world has continually been at war or engaging in domestic civil wars.

Why?

Perhaps it takes repeated wars to reeducate generation by generation those who cannot imagine the reality of war and civil war.

In school, I was taught history chronologically, war by war, and how the victors carved new national boundaries and subjugated the vanquished only to have domestic revolutions subdivide countries.

After wars or revolutions end in battlefields and graveyards, but after that generation dies off, wars become books or movies or heroic stories.

It is all just "book learning." It's easy to get good grades and learn nothing.

After my formal education was over, museums, libraries and good conversations became my continuing education; but international travel gave me the best insights into my own country, its prosperity and its people.

Over ten years ago, I spent an evening with friends in a beautiful plaza in Aleppo in Northern Syria. Talk about the government was discouraged by our guide. Less than a year later, Syria was at war with itself and that beautiful plaza and much of the city had been wiped off the face of the earth.

A little further south, the 2,000-year-old Roman ruins of Palmera, a once beautiful city built around a long dry oasis, would be badly damaged by this modern war.

When I visited Dubrovnik more recently, our guide pointed out the bullet holes that had chipped away that walled city, which had been part of the former nation state of Yugoslavia.

Last summer, during a trip to northern France and the battlefields of the First World War, our guide at the Battle of Belleau Wood pointed to a stand of trees and asked, "How could these trees have survived the battles here and the later deforestation that cleared these fields around it?" And then answered: "The fighting here was so severe that the trees cannot be cut down because the bullets still buried in these trees would break the blades of the saws."

I have also visited cities and nation-states torn by war and revolution, for example, when I visited the occupied and divided Beirut, Lebanon.

I had been invited to an opulent lunch overlooking a beautiful beach and the city below.

In the cab home, the driver spoke some English. In stop-and-go traffic we were delayed at a roundabout. I found myself three feet from the barrel of a tank pointing directly at my face.

Hoping to encourage the driver to edge forward slightly, I started a conversation, asking about a billboard with a cornucopia of figures looking down on me. He told me that it memorialized the assassinated leaders of the country and city.

That evening, I had dinner with a family who had lived on the top floor of an apartment building in another section of the city, which had had its roof blown off during the intermittent shelling of the city the year before.

A teenage member of the family joked that his mother had, after the damage of the blast, asked if everyone in the family was all right and then went back to eating dinner.

When I asked how on earth they could be so matter of fact, he answered, "Dinner was ready and getting cold." He then added that fighting had been going on and off in various parts of the city for years, and when it was near their school they got days off until the fighting moved elsewhere.

On my way to the airport as I headed back to the U.S. the next day, I had to show my passport to soldiers in the quadrant of the city that held the airport. I can't remember if they were Shia or Sunni.

So what does global history teach me about my country?

"It can't happen here."

Our country supports the freedom fighters of Ukraine as they fight and die to preserve their country from the bloody invasion by Putin — the autocrat so admired by our former president.

After the failed coup d'état lead by this former president (who then raised a quarter of a billion dollars selling the false claim of a stolen election), almost every member of his party voted against an investigation of that coup. Now, half our country still refuses to acknowledge the January 6th Committee's findings, even though almost all the witnesses are Republicans appointed by Republicans.

The most important protector of a democracy is the informed voter. I wish many of my fellow Americans could be as fortunate as I have been, getting to travel internationally.

So many of my friends will tell me, "We have always gotten through it before. We're Americans. It can't happen here."

"It can't happen here."

Long Ago:
A Tale in Two Sonnets

Almost three decades ago, on November 29, 1995, I visited the Mayan city of Tikal before its restoration, with two stoners I didn't know:

Belief

The stars over Tikal are frightening and bright.
I am here, on sacred land, in the jungle
Before dawn in the Guatemalan night.
The moisture and pre-morning has its smell

But I modernize the scent with smoke
From a little match to start my cigarette.
Cesar comes through the door drinking a coke.
He says he knew the others would all forget.

He won't take me into the ruins alone.
Down the dark path, I follow my flashlight
Into the past, to where time has made its home
And into the temple and sacrificial sites

Where people of belief played their cosmic part
And reached through ribs to hold high a human heart.

Many years later I went back to show my daughter, but it was now open to tourists:

Returning to Tikal with My Daughter

The exchanging of colored currency
As soldiers lounged and smoked their cigarettes
While an old woman washed clothes in the stream
Should have been enough to never forget,

But I wanted to show her so much more.
We crossed the bridge into Guatemala
And into the land of the living poor.
Skinny dogs and pigs with hanging teats wallow

In the roadside brush as we both bus by.
Not even Tikal, ancient in starlight,
In its totalitarian demise
Got the primal message exactly right

But heading home, past pack boys with a load
A twelve-foot Boa stretched across the road.

The Older You Get the Shorter Your Stories Should Be

Redemption and a Big Divot in World History

It is almost impossible to describe the First World War in simple terms. It is unresolved as to how it evolved into the war it became — the number of casualties it caused easily exceeds eight million dead and double that in maimed and wounded — and its end probably was the beginning of the Second World War only twenty years later. Books and books and books continue to be written about it. It is a wellspring of scholarship and a mirror for the future and present.

There are two things it demonstrates to me, however. First, we seem to be incapable of maturing at the same speed as our ability to make weapons evermore capable of our mass destruction. Second, we seem to be able to commit ourselves blindly to use these weapons without realizing the extent of the destruction that we can cause. Both of these observations demonstrate the incredible capacity we have in the form of the "nation state" to destroy ourselves, despite our individual capacity to feel compassion, empathy, and kindness for each other on a daily basis as human beings who are not in a state of war.

Why have I featured a picture of a crater?

WWI introduced airplane warfare, submarine warfare, the machine gun, the tank, and gas warfare. The warfare was so intense that there are specific monuments dedicated to both missing soldiers and unidentifiable body parts.

So, is there something, a simple example from this war, that demonstrates redemption? Yes, I think there is.

Both sides built tunnels for days and months for incredible distances under entire towns and enemy lines to set explosives. Some of these tunnels were only four feet wide and three-and-a-half feet high. The excavation of the dirt was extremely difficult and endlessly time consuming. Imagine the commitment. Imagine the claustrophobia. Imagine the amount of explosives that then had to be carried underground to blow up a town or an enemy stronghold.

As I have said, the picture I have provided is of a crater. It is thirty to forty feet deep and almost a football field wide. The explosion sent debris four thousand feet in the air and killed and injured people who were never found. I took the photograph from the far side. There is a monument on the other side which, if you look closely, is a cross that is several stories high.

In the alternative, it has been documented that during a one-day armistice for Christmas the soldiers from both sides came out over their trenches, exchanged chocolate and cigarettes, and sang Christmas carols together.

Back to the Future

Recently, I took a trip because I wanted to "feel" what it was like to live in WWII Germany and the Soviet Cold War occupation in Czechoslovakia and Poland.

I already knew the dates, places and times from textbooks, but it's quite different to experience what it was like to have lived during those times.

Of course, the trip would come alive in museums and, unexpectedly, it brought back for me a long lost feeling I had years ago when I was just a young boy. I had gotten lost offshore in Buzzards Bay in a small motorboat that was running out of gas on an outgoing tide in thick predawn fog.

It is odd how we learn through memories and association.

How odd that museums, which were about imprisonment, brought back the feeling of drifting out to sea, creating an odd claustrophobia without barriers other than an endless borderless fog.

The claustrophobia slowly kicked in when I visited Checkpoint Charlie, the famous heavily guarded passthrough in the Berlin Wall, which kept the East Germans imprisoned inside.

It started with a set of pictures of a boy who had scrambled to climb the wall in an effort to live in freedom, but the photos chronicled how he had died riddled with bullets, hanging from barbed razor wire near the top of the wall.

How odd that I could feel claustrophobic under wide-open skies?

A few days later, the claustrophobia increased in one of the East German museums that focused on the Nazi SS and their little gray bread trucks. These had no windows, just a sliding door on one side and three closet-sized cells so small that prisoners could not stand but only sit in a narrow chair, hands by their sides, while they were taken to a concentration camp somewhere outside of Berlin.

A few days later as we traveled toward Prague, we stopped at another prison that was three or four stories high with interrogation cells on the top floor. The inmates who would not answer were showed pictures of their family who would be killed if they continued to resist.

Putin had spent six months in the house across the street when he was in Soviet intelligence, attempting to flip the tortured inmates to become Soviet spies.

The claustrophobia wrapped around me in that silent building when I realized what it must have felt like day and night in there. It was missing the noise of slamming cell doors, the echoing screams and the smell of the single bucket in the corner, which acted as a bathroom in each cramped cell, with three to a single bed and no mattress.

I know now why the feeling I had on this trip was claustrophobic, but I thought it was still an odd reaction to the history of the past until I realized I had lived my whole life free in a democracy.

All of a sudden, I felt imprisonment under borderless wide-open skies as a psychological imprisonment which became unbearable.

All of a sudden, I could feel the last breath of the boy crucified and bleeding from razor wire on the top of a Berlin Wall as a reaction to my claustrophobia and his death.

Years ago, as I slowly ran out of gas in my little boat, I saw the outline of a cliff as the late morning fog broke. There were connected ladders and a climbing set of stairs. I beached the boat and climbed to the top of the cliff and knocked on the door of a little cottage overlooking the ocean.

A woman with the Sunday newspaper tucked under her arm answered the door. I breathlessly asked, "Where am I?" She looked at me quizzically and answered "Menemsha," then paused, "Martha's Vineyard," and then paused again… "The United States of America."

I remember feeling happy and alive.

The World We Choose to Make

I have not posted a blog in the last three weeks because I have been to hell and back. I traveled to the darkest place I've ever been, and then returned to a place of joy, laughter, love and light.

I went on a trip through World War II in Germany, Czechoslovakia, and Poland, and then returned to witness my son's wedding and its explosion of joy.

History as dates, places and times is taught and graded, but only the imagination can bring it to life and give it meaning.

In Poland, at the end of our trip, I went to Auschwitz, the concentration camp.

Auschwitz had the most efficient business plan I have ever seen.

I stood at the exact location where the trains emptied and a guard made an instantaneous decision, pointing left or right. To the right went the children and their mothers (if their mothers could not work), destined for the gas chambers. To the left went men and women who could be worked to death. Their life expectancy was pre-calculated to be three months. Excess food was not wasted on them since there was an endless supply of new labor coming off the trains each day. They killed thousands upon thousands of these people each week.

Inside the camp today, there are multiple display cases. Behind the glass of the display cases are piles of clothes, shoes or pots and pans, which had been carried by the executed. In one display case, among the scattered clothing, there was a little pair of red children's shoes unbuckled. In another, a perfectly intact three-foot-long braid of hair cut from the scalp of a young child. It had a light blue bow still in place at the end.

It seemed impossible to me that the neighborhoods of little country houses outside the camp did not know what was happening in there as the trains rolled in and crematoriums belched smoke that fouled the air. Could they not hear the cries of children as their parents were separated from them, or of the families who came to realize that they were not being taken to a safe place outside of Germany as promised but were living their last moments before they would die?

I was reminded of a time when I was still practicing law, when I was hired to represent a slaughterhouse in a zoning dispute. The slaughterhouse was comprised of two buildings in a suburban neighborhood in Baltimore County.

There was a little house where the business offices were located, and there was a two-story building, which had a ramp that zigzagged up to a door where three cows were lined up head to tail, waiting in line motionless.

The slaughterhouse owners were Christians, and I was introduced to a rabbi who was hired to ensure that the process was kosher. I was given the tour of the site in preparation for the trial, and I traveled up the ramp that held the three cows and then into the building. I remember doing a double take as I noticed the eyes of the lead cow. I saw that they were wide-eyed and afraid.

Inside the door, I passed the carcasses, which had been stripped of their skin and hung swaying on hooks headless as they were carried by a conveyor belt to the efficient butchers, who cut the meat into steaks, filets, rib roasts, and further down the line, ground beef.

Two days later, I returned from Europe and flew to Houston, where I presided over the rehearsal dinner celebrating my son's wedding the following day.

The bridesmaids had known each other since high school. Months before, they had celebrated common birthdays together on a weeklong trip to Paris. They were destined to be lifelong friends. My son's friends had also gone to school or college together and shared comparable deep friendships. The joy and humor of this collective group as they mingled the day before the wedding was palpable and full of laughter and love and friendship on so many levels.

After the wedding ended, the bride and groom traveled into their new life down a runway that was lined on both sides with family and friends holding sparklers.

On the flight home from the wedding, I could not forget the story I was told by our guide at Auschwitz when I asked, "did anyone ever escape?" He replied, "Only the Polish prisoners would occasionally get away because Auschwitz was in a Polish neighborhood where the prisoners could disappear and be exported out of hell by their friends."

Courage

"The Believers" and "the Nonbelievers"

Recently, I was fortunate to spend two weeks in southern Africa in the bush in a zoo without borders. After a long flight from New York to South Africa and a relatively short flight to Victoria Falls in Zimbabwe, a small group of fellow travelers and I flew in several single engine planes and later three helicopters to a wonderful, elegant resort campsite, miles from everywhere deep in Botswana.

Botswana is about the size of Texas, has a population of about two million people, and has reserved approximately 37% of its land for the preservation of its natural habitat.

The first thing you notice as the dawn comes up on the first day is how wide the sky is. As you scan it you notice that the clouds offer several widely different configurations and weather patterns. Then you realize how big the land is beneath the sky and how far away you are from everybody else.

Slightly before dawn, during breakfast on the first day, we are told explicitly that the jeeps that we will be riding in have no sides and, as long as we stay within the boundaries of the jeep, we will not be attacked by any of the animals. The animals are apparently not threatened by the jeeps, which they perceive as foul-smelling mechanical elephants that neither attack the animals nor are worthy of their attack. That is the basis for our safety.

However, we were informed, if we get out of the jeep it is an entirely different game. We are told that within the last two years in South Africa a photographer who leaned out of one of the jeeps for a better photograph was attacked by a lion and when the guide tried to save her, he was also killed.

The first morning as we leave the campsite we travel into the bush and see huge herds of zebras and impalas living in fear of the lions that stalk them, but we see no lions. The second morning, just after dawn, we turn into a small clearing and are confronted by four lions walking slowly toward us from a distance of about 50 yards. The driver stops the jeep and instructs us to say nothing but feel free to photograph. The lions slowly and methodically move toward us. We are facing them and they are walking our way.

As the lions slowly approach, my fellow riders in the jeep become either "believers" that the jeep is safe territory or "nonbelievers" who, with every step of the lions, seem to be counting down the last seconds of their lives. They can't move and the fear becomes palpable. The eyes are wide and the breathing becomes slightly labored.

On the other hand, the believers are happily photographing and silently adjusting their telescopic lenses. The lions grow closer and closer and, within 10 feet, three veer to the right and one veers to the left so that it will be behind us. Everyone in the jeep recognizes that they must keep their eyes on the three lions that will pass to our left within several feet of the jeep, but we will not be able to turn and watch the one lion that is moving behind us on our right.

The believers continue to happily photograph adjusting their telescopic lens to catch the reflection of the jeep in a lion's eyes. The nonbelievers are breathing softly, their eyes closed, waiting for death.

After a few moments they were past us and we started the engine and continued our day.

Photo: Salim Virji; CC BY-SA 2.0

Fear Separates Heroes from Cowards

Fear separates heroes from cowards.

I live in beautiful northern Baltimore County west of Harford County, north of Baltimore city and south of the Pennsylvania line. It is rich with beautiful horse farms, deer and fox hunting, verdant farmland and wonderful people.

I am a moderate Democrat. Where I live is by and large Trump country but I love my neighbors. For the most part, we don't let politics get in the way of respect and friendship.

Last week, two friends and I held a small fundraiser for a Democratic Congressional candidate who is running to unseat an incumbent Trump Republican who met in the White House to plan the January 6th attack on the Capital.

As the midterms have been approaching, for some reason, I have been remembering old litigation from when I had been hired by a prominent personal injury lawyer to try the cases he thought he would lose.

In the 1980s, the Harford County Courthouse was being renovated. An alternative courthouse annex was set up to handle cases while the renovations proceeded.

This temporary courthouse had a makeshift heating, air conditioning and ventilation system hung from the ceiling, and the sounds from other courtrooms and the neighboring bathroom could be heard through this system during the proceedings.

I had been assigned a case which my employer had said was "difficult." Our client, a young-for-his-age teenage boy, was so shy he could barely answer my questions about his bicycle accident during our first meeting.

The accident involved a car and the boy had his leg broken and his bicycle destroyed. There were real questions about who was at fault. His parents filed on his behalf and, without his knowledge, a lawsuit for extensive damages.

The boy had no friends and was so shy that his only freedom came when he left school in the afternoon to ride his bike for hours along country roads while his classmates played seasonal team sports.

His parents were clearly disappointed by their son. He would never be the football captain or the class president.

I met him with his parents for trial preparation about a week before trial. After we went over the case that had been filed, the boy seemed reticent, and I asked his parents to leave the room. I asked him to go over the facts once more with me one on one. He looked down and repeated what his parents had told me before they had left the room. He was uncomfortable, but what was striking about him was that when his eyes met mine and he told me something, he was honest, definitive, and straightforward.

I feared this was a boy who was being forced to tell a story instead of the truth.

He clearly was not looking forward to testifying under oath.

On the day of trial, I asked his parents to bring him to the courthouse early so that he could sit in the witness chair alone without anybody there, to familiarize himself with the space and settle his nerves.

When he sat alone in that witness chair he was terrified. I wanted his parents to see him sitting there alone staring into space and shaking before anybody else came into that courtroom.

I then asked him to go sit with his parents so we could talk about the possibility that the case could be settled before trial. The parents refused and reiterated that they wanted several hundred thousand dollars in damages.

Several minutes later, the opposing counsel came in and started to set up for the trial. Shortly thereafter, the people who would be chosen as jurors filtered in.

The boy had become more and more frightened. About 10 minutes before the judge would appear and we would pick a jury, the boy slowly started to cry by himself. I noticed that the parents were trying to cover this up, and they asked to remove him briefly from the courtroom to go to the bathroom so he could compose himself.

The defense counsel had offered nothing to settle the case, because he believed that the boy was too shy to make a good impression before the jury. He ambled over and offered a nominal amount to resolve the case, which is not unusual before a case begins.

All of a sudden, through the heating ducts from the bathroom, the sound of gagging and then a toilet repeatedly flushing could be heard.

The defense counsel asked where the boy was. I said I was sure he would be back before the judge entered and we started picking a jury.

Moments later, the boy's father came into the courtroom and signaled for me to join him in the hall. He told me the boy had refused to testify but his father instructed me that he was going to make sure he did.

I asked the father to consider a settlement of the case, because the boy clearly was uncomfortable with testifying to something that apparently he did not believe was true. The father said he would consult his wife. I insisted that whatever decision was made had to be given to me by my client, their son.

He hurried off to the bathroom and returned with his wife who agreed that the boy would be ready to testify.

I told them to get their son. They told me to come into the men's room because he wouldn't leave his stall.

The boy looked at me when he came out of the stall, tears streaming down his face. He looked down and wouldn't talk. I looked at him and said, do you want me to resolve this case? And he nodded. His parents objected. I push them aside. What do you think is a fair settlement, I asked. He waved his hands as if to say nothing. I told him that the other side had made a nominal offer to merely resolve the case and I asked him whether I could negotiate further and resolve it rather than dismiss it. His parents resisted, but he nodded yes.

When I reentered the courtroom the sound of the toilet flushing was coming through the ductwork and there were muffled heated voices also coming through.

The defense counsel asked again where my client was. The judge was about to enter. I joked that if he only had offered a little more money, maybe it could have been resolved. He added to his offer. I told him I was authorized to settle the case for double that amount and we did.

It wasn't much. It was a compromise. Enough to pay some hospital bills and get a replacement bicycle for the boy.

It only took about 10 or 15 minutes to put the settlement on the record and send the jury home. I left the courthouse and looked for the boy and his parents. Their car was gone, and I never saw them again.

I wish I could have said goodbye to that boy who was too shy to confront the world, but had the courage to stand his ground and refuse to lie!

Fear separates the heroes from the cowards.

Two days ago, after our little political fundraiser, my friend and his wife, who had held the reception at their home, woke up to find a dead fox hung from their mailbox.

This is not who we are in northern Baltimore County.

This is not who we are as Americans.

The Older You Get the Shorter Your Stories Should Be

How the Definition of Courage Changes

As a young man my heroes proved their courage by welcoming and taking on great risk. I am amazed at how my heroes have changed over time.

In a few days, Susan and I will fly to the Osa Peninsula and the rainforest of southwestern Costa Rica. This will be the first trip there for Susan, but for me it will be a reunion with a place where I experienced real fear for the first time in my life.

In the late 1980s, I decided to go to Costa Rica to find the deepest rainforest I could find. I wanted an adventure and to be left alone.

I flew to San José, spent the night, and got a little plane to fly me to a grass runway. There, I met a crazy American expat who would transport me in his little boat down a muddy river to the Pacific, and then south along the virgin jungle coastline to a remote lodge he had put together in the Corcovado rain forest.

The place was run by a small family for the expat. I knew I was in for a great adventure because the expat had a huge untrimmed beard and claimed he had a wife in Texas and a wife in Costa Rica and immediately told me, quite confidentiality, that he was an operative for the CIA. He had some issues. The place was empty except for me during the entire week I was there.

That is where I met Rafael, the teenage son of the farming family that managed the place when it was not the rainy season. He was assigned to take me fishing and scuba diving in a tiny Boston whaler.

Rafael had to pump the scuba tanks with a gas-powered compressor and catch our bait before we went out each morning to dive to find shark caves, fish offshore past Caño Island, or to go up the rivers to live within a world of howler monkeys that threw sticks at us from above and massive blue morpho butterflies and macaws that flew around us as we traveled into the rainforest.

Rafael did not like diving because he was afraid of sharks, which he claimed had killed a married couple the year before. I fashioned myself as a bit of a daredevil, so I told him I was not afraid.

On my last day there, I told Rafael he could go wherever he wanted and I would go with him. Neither of us knew the other's language but he told me he wanted to fish for giant pargo offshore, way out past the island, where the drop-off brought the big fish to feed in the current. All we had was light tackle. These fish can grow to as much as 40 pounds and tend to go deep and run. I'm pretty sure that Rafael did not share with his parents what we were going to do.

We packed extra water and cold beer and some sandwiches. He brought an extra tank of gas. We left in the late morning and easily caught several mackerel for bait. Rafael cut them in half and secured them on our hooks as we motored out into the Pacific. We went way out further than we had gone before. When I lost sight of land for the first time, I became a little afraid. After a while, Rafael switched the gas tanks.

I was at the bow of the boat and Rafael was back at the motor. We sat silently for several hours without a bite. As the sun started to go down, I wanted to go home. We had not seen land for a couple of hours by now. I became a little more afraid as we drifted with the current, but I kept it to myself.

As the dark came, I turned to look at him, but his rod was bent over and, when he looked back, he grinned and said one word: "Grande!"

The fish was running deeper and deeper and heading further out into the Pacific. Now I was frightened, but told myself it could be I was just out of my element and I should trust Rafael.

Rafael, on his unexpected day off, was too excited to give in to the fish. The stars started to come out and we kept being pulled out to sea. The night came, and Rafael kept reeling in the fish and then letting more line go out until there was no line left but his giant fish would not tire as it kept pulling us deeper and deeper into the dark.

The sea was calm and, with the dark, I had no sense of which direction the land was anymore. The moon rose in the night sky. There was a blanket of bright stars above us now and nothing but silence and the lapping of the gentle waves against the side of the boat until the line broke.

As we prepared to go, we threw the remaining mackerel overboard and the phosphorus all around lit up as our discarded bait was devoured by surface fish.

Rafael pulled the cord to start the boat, but it wouldn't start. He tried and tried again without success. We had already used the extra tank of gas to get us out there. We were drifting in the dark with the stars above us as we were taken by the tide.

I was deeply afraid, but was I wrong to be? I didn't think so.

Rafael tried and tried until finally there was a sputtering, but the engine died. Then he tried once more and it started. Rafael cautiously revved the engine several times and, after examining the stars, he turned the boat and headed toward what I hoped was home.

Despite it all, it was stunningly beautiful. As we skimmed across the water for more than an hour, we lit up the phosphorus around us. Dolphins joined us on both sides of the boat with the glowing phosphorus trailing behind us as we careened over the water with the stars stretched over our heads.

Rafael kept checking the stars.

I was certain we were lost but Rafael refused to show fear. Was I overreacting? Finally, a dim light appeared in a shadow that must be the edge of the rain forest. The lights of the little lodge were all on and there were flashlights coming from the little dock.

As we got closer, I could see several people standing silently on the dock holding the flashlights and pointing them out at the sea. We had no running lights so it appeared they were guiding us in. We slowed the boat and pulled up to the little ladder.

I felt foolish that I had been so afraid and accepted the hands offered to me as I climbed the ladder and stood on the dock.

Rafael tied up the boat and when he climbed the ladder his mother greeted him and slapped him harder than I've ever seen anybody hit before in my life. His family had been waiting ever since the sun went down. I was later told it had been hours of uncertainty.

When I visit Costa Rica this time, I am sure that the virgin rainforest will have other lodges now, but I have also changed. My heroes now are common people as they almost invisibly care for others.

I have come to understand better now the fear that boy's mother felt as she waited on the dock in the night and shined her flashlight out at the sea.

Photo: Susan Chase

In Search of a Lost Friend

As I anticipated our visit to the southwestern Costa Rican rainforests, I remembered a fishing trip I had taken from a solitary lodge down there over 35 years ago with a guide named Rafael.

We had become friends back then because we took risks and, on the day before I left, shared an incredible, terrifying adventure. We went way out into the Pacific and into the night in a little Boston Whaler and almost didn't find our way back.

But people get lost when you get sucked back into the day-to-day and the years compound.

A friend suggested I try to find Rafael on this trip. I decided to try to find Rafael if I could. It was a real long shot. All I had was his first name. Would he still be there? Would he even remember me? Was he even alive? Basque del Cabo, the wonderful place where Susan and I are staying, is about two hours south of Drake Bay where I met Rafael.

Yesterday, we flew south from San José to the little air strip at Puerto Jiménez and were picked up by a four-wheel drive Jeep to go further south to our destination.

Could I even find a way to get to Drake Bay if I found him?

On the ride, I recited my story of my trip thirty-five years ago to our driver and asked if there was any chance we could locate Rafael after all these years. The idea piqued his interest and he volunteered to get me to Drake Bay if we could locate Rafael.

When we arrived at the lodge, I told my story again to the owner and he also was intrigued and immediately called on his assistant to see what she could find.

After some preliminary research, they told me what I expected. The expat who owned the place I had stayed in at Drake Bay had died and the place had been sold but was still around. Over the last thirty-five years, a few other lodges were constructed on Drake Bay. Perhaps Rafael had stayed to helped build them and was still around.

Yesterday after breakfast, I was told they thought that they had found Rafael but were waiting for confirmation. If they have the right Rafael, he worked as a carpenter to help build the new properties. He was about 55 years old, but they had not determined if he was still living down near the bay. They said this man had a son who was a cab driver in San José. Perhaps he had moved up there.

Before we left Maryland, I had asked myself how we might recognize each other, and it occurred to me that I had saved the raggedy old lion shirt in which I had fished and scuba-dived and pretty much lived in down there. I photographed it and packed it just in case I thought I found him.

The assistant continued to make calls and emailed these new lodges over the next few days, but we were still not able to locate him.

With only three days to go, I booked an offshore fishing trip out of Puerto Jiménez to make my own inquiries about Rafael, and to determine how far we really had gone out to sea before we lost sight of land that day and night.

We left around seven o'clock from Puerto Jiménez in a covered boat about three times the size of the Boston whaler Rafael had used. The captain was about 35 and his mate was about the same age as Rafael was when we went out to sea years ago.

There was only one other boat going out that morning. The two were in radio contact in search of tuna and sailfish throughout the morning. We watched for the gathering of birds diving into the ocean, feeding off squid or schools of fish driven to the surface by the dolphins. These schools would bring the tuna and sailfish, which we wanted to catch.

It was a beautiful day. The cumulonimbus clouds climbed into the sky over the shoreline as we traveled out on a slow rolling tide. Around 11:30, we hooked an 80-pound yellowfin tuna that took about 25 minutes to land.

The shoreline was still visible at 10 miles out. I asked about Rafael, but the captain didn't really know anyone all that well as far north as Drake Bay.

Before we left, I had asked the resort owner's assistant to keep trying to locate Rafael. My time was running out. I had only one more day before we had to leave at 5:15 in the morning to get on the only plane leaving Puerto Jiménez for San José, take the mandatory Covid test at 8:00 to ensure we could return home on our 2:30 p.m. Delta flight.

As we arrived at the dock to meet our ride back to the lodge, I was surprised to see the assistant there. After we loaded the tuna into the back of the truck, the assistant was strangely quiet as she rode in the passenger seat next to the driver. From the backseat I asked if she had been able to set up our meeting at Drake Bay. She paused, turned her face toward me, and winced as she looked back at me. "He is dead."

After the long and bumpy ride back to the lodge, I asked Susan, "Wouldn't it be easy just to lie about that?"

I decided I would pay our bill early, rather than the next morning. I wanted some time with the assistant so I could cross examine her indirectly about the seriousness of her inquiries.

When we met, she went very carefully over the bill and the tips we had designated for the staff. She meticulously double-checked the math in a way that sadly made me realize how careful and professional she was.

I asked her about what her most recent research had revealed and she confirmed the care that she had put into trying to find Rafael. She pulled out her phone and played back the voicemail reply from an old guide who had retired from her work in Drake Bay years ago. The assistant translated each sentence into English as she played it back.

The caller explained she had been in the back of a taxi cab in San José several years ago with a driver who asked where she was from. When she said Drake Bay, the driver told her he had grown up there. He said his father was a carpenter who had built several buildings as they went up around Drake Bay, including the first lodge that had been constructed there in 1985. His father and mother were one of the first families to populate the southwestern stretch of the Pacific and rainforest around Drake Bay. His father's name was Rafael.

I told the assistant I would be willing to meet the cabdriver at the Delta terminal in San José after my Covid test. I would feed him lunch and also give him about $100 in colóns as a friend of his father in the hopes that he would meet me. She agreed to keep trying.

The next morning, we did the Covid test, and checked the bags, but I did not go through security at the international airport. I sat on the floor next to the Delta desk.

I waited and waited until there was no time left. I went through security and as I boarded the plane to leave, I gave my remaining Costa Rican currency to an unsuspecting vendor and asked nothing in return.

It is so easy to lose people and so hard to find them.

Even if I had been successful, I'm sure his son would have pocketed the money and returned to his cab and his daily life.

Thirty-five years ago, there was something courageous and determined about Rafael's refusal to cut the line and return to safety — and I had refused to stop him.

Looking out the plane window as we took off, I thought even when he is completely forgotten he will be safe and respected in my memory.

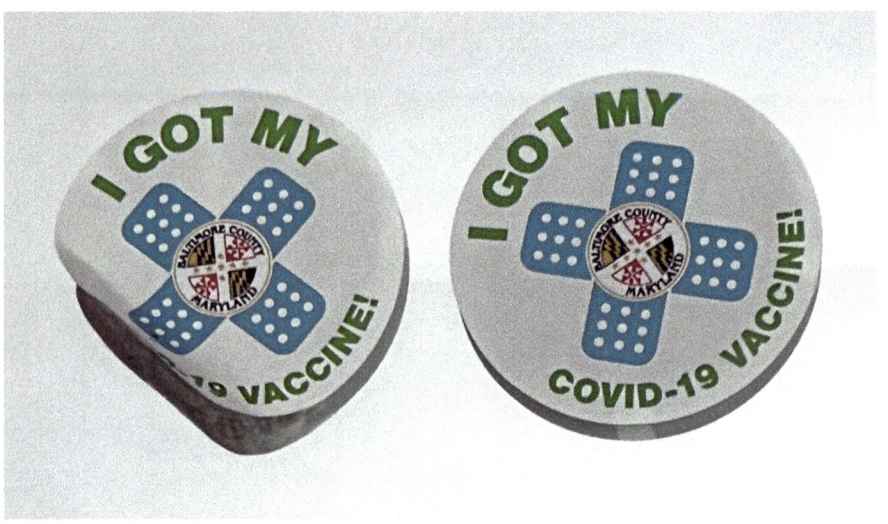

Let's Get This Party Started

"*The whole aim of practical politics is to keep the populace alarmed (and hence clamorous to be led to safety) by menacing it with an endless series of hobgoblins, all of them imaginary.*" — H. L. Mencken

September 12th is H. L. Mencken's birthday. He was a wonderful, provocative, opinionated *Baltimore Sun* columnist who was definitely not politically correct and loved to piss off everybody.

Though I could never match him, the only way to celebrate him is to follow his lead. Please accept this as all in good fun.

Extra! Extra! Read all about it! Where in the Constitution is the freedom of choice?

"*Democracy is the theory that the common people know what they want, and deserve to get it good and hard.*" — H. L. Mencken

Let us first consider American "freedom of choice," which has been heavily relied on by anti-vaxxers and the intellectuals on Fox News.

Let's start with a little history. In the mid-1950s, my mother joined all the other mothers back then who lined up their children for the new polio vaccine and thereafter for mumps, measles and who knows what, including all kinds of booster shots. It was so long ago there were "pin cushion" jokes. (Back then, people had sewing machines and pin cushions.)

Yes! These were the days when tattooed people were not afraid of needles, and vaccinations were not considered to be secret government DNA changes.

It wasn't perfect, but I am sure that many of us are alive today because our "Rosie the Riveter" mothers, fresh from their patriotic duties and the sacrifices of the Second World War, grabbed their first-graders and put them in line.

It was a civic duty that their children were safe and also not spreading any infectious diseases. I guess today they would be blamed for not looking out for number one.

This is not to say I have given up on the present.

I was very happy when almost every anti-vaxxer I talked to refused to tell me where this "freedom of choice" is located in the Constitution. But was saddened that nonetheless they said it was "in there someplace."

Unfortunately, after a careful review of the Constitution, I discovered that "freedom of choice" is, in fact, from a short-lived Burger King commercial campaign. The fact that it was short-lived seems to indicate that most of these Americans preferred uniformity in their Whoppers.

When I argued that perhaps freedom of choice at least requires a concern for others, and it was inappropriate to disseminate misinformation, citing my mother as an example, I got nowhere.

For my back-up authority for both proposals, I asked If they recognized these names: Marc Bernier, Dick Farrel, Tod Tucker, Jimmy DeYoung Sr., and Phil Valentine. I pointed out that they had two things in common: they have all made a fortune as anti-vaxxer talk show hosts and they all have died of Covid. I can't even imagine how many people they took with them.

Even George Washington, the father of our country, recognized the need to sacrifice some freedoms for the greater good. He had his entire regiment inocculated against smallpox which, along with other diseases, was killing more of the contintental army than the redcoats. We may not have had a country if not for the modern medicine of 1776.

Of course, I could be wrong about all of this. Just ask Mencken:

"There is always an easy solution to every problem — neat, plausible, and wrong." — H. L. Mencken

Henry Louis Mencken was born in 1880, so on September 12th he would have been 141 years old and almost half the age of our country. So, let's get this party started!

"If, after I depart this vale, you ever remember me and have thought to please my ghost, forgive some sinner and wink your eye at some homely girl." — H. L. Mencken

He was politically incorrect but he still can shock you and make you laugh. Happy Birthday to the man who always gave 'em H. L.

Photo: Susan Chase

My Heart Is Broken but I Saw Love

I have always been a soft touch when it comes to animals. It has gotten me in trouble and on occasion broken my heart.

My heart is broken today but it has also been reawakened.

Many years ago, I was driving past Towson University when I saw a baby raccoon abandoned near the entrance. She looked sick and starving. Without hesitation, I pulled the car over.

She was curled up and about the size of my hand. She was probably only a week old and was all alone, so of course I scooped her up, named her Thomas Jefferson, and took her home. I got instructions from a vet and fed her with a dropper.

I became so attached over that first week that I set my alarm to ensure her steady feedings, and when she died very late one night I, without a second thought, gave her artificial respiration.

My wife was justifiably horrified and insisted I get a rabies shot, which I did. Thereafter the joke in the neighborhood was, "If you see a rabid animal, call Bob because he can bite back."

My animal advocacy and militant, often imprudent, protection of animals was acquired early. When I was about nine or ten, I lived next to a high school which held a "Sportsman's Show" to raise money.

Somebody had blown up a wading pool and put 100 trout in it so that the "sportsmen" could use barbed treble hooks to snag the trout, which were then promptly cleaned and taken home to be fried.

I was horrified by the cruelty and the thought that every one of these trout was doomed.

I went back home to my piggy bank. I returned with money and a net to buy three trout with my savings, but I did not want them killed.

I had a plan.

I filled up the bathtub in the third floor of our house, placed the trout in it and refused to take a bath until my parents drove my fish to be released in New Hampshire. After a week and a half of no baths, my parents became persuaded.

It got worse.

Back then, if you went to the circus, you could buy chameleons which had little strings around their necks and a safety pin to clip them to your shirt. They didn't stand a chance.

I again emptied my piggy bank to buy as many chameleons as I could, and then housed them in an old aquarium. I built a landscaped jungle with little waterfalls and a window screen top for air circulation. That summer, I traveled with a tiny little fish net, so I could catch live flies for food. I concluded that the pet store food was not good enough for them. It was less organic than my free-range flies.

It got worse.

I cared for a small alligator that was shipped to me from Florida back when that was legal, and it lived in my bathtub until I, again, convinced my parents that life would be better for it at the zoo.

It got worse.

There were birds with broken wings, which I fed all of the bay scallops that were scheduled for dinner. There were these two kittens that I acquired while hitchhiking, when somebody had fed them both LSD so they were anxiously fighting hallucinations. I named them Fruehauf and Brockway, the names of trucking companies.

One summer, we rented a house on Maryland's Eastern Shore, and my job was to care for a pregnant cat that lived in a woodpile in the barn. Of course I was there when the nine kittens were born. I spent the rest of the summer forever getting them back to their mother in the woodpile.

Over time, my parents gave in and we adopted a black stray female mixed breed who, of course, jumped the fence and had three puppies in the garage.

When I met my second wife over a decade ago, she had a one-year-old puppy named Winston, which made me love her even more. Several months ago, Winston developed tumors and problems with his lungs and hind legs. Last week, we were told by our vet that Winston had only two or three months left.

My wife and I were scheduled to visit her family in Florida last weekend, but the vet told us that even though Winston could last for a few more months, it would be too stressful to board him at her kennel, given the stress and his condition. I volunteered to stay home with Winston so my wife could be with her family. Unexpectedly, Winston went into decline, and we decided the only humane thing to do was to put him down as soon as possible.

I was up several times throughout Sunday night to give Winston painkillers. The doctor came at 10:00 in the morning yesterday, sedated Winston, and then administered the shot. After we waited, she gently took out her stethoscope and softly pronounced him dead.

Winston knew my wife longer than I have, and they loved each other dearly. When she decided to put him down, even though she couldn't be there, I recognized it was a sacrifice for her. There were tears, but she said she cared more for the quality of his life than for the pain she would feel not getting to see him one last time.

It is one thing to love animals, but it is another when you see the humanity of someone who sacrifices their feelings for those they love.

The Practice of Law

Taking Flight

Way before I started my own business law firm in 1990, I was hired to be an associate by a group of lawyers who didn't like each other.

My job, at that time in my career, was to litigate all the bad cases in the office, particularly if the client was a friend of one of the partners.

One of the first partners I met was also an amateur pilot who had taken out a loan with a friend to buy an airplane. Innocently, in an effort to fit in, I remarked that I hoped I could someday learn to fly. The partner immediately sensed blood in the water. He suggested I buy a one-third interest in the new airplane, and also co-sign the loan with him.

I had convinced myself to get licensed to fly in an airplane that I didn't want but I had just bought.

It got worse.

I soon learned that the lawyer's friend and co-owner of my new airplane had so many creditors that he had no bank accounts, and all business was done from a big roll of bills which bulged in his pocket.

He could make anybody laugh. He could make everyone like him. He was one of those down-to-earth-aggressively-friendly-I've-got-nothing-to-hide kind of guys, so he immediately was candid about the large polyps he said were way up his nose. If anyone questioned him on this subject he would start snorting loudly until they laughed and then he'd spit into a trash can.

He could also deflect any questions about the wad of cash in his pocket. He would answer that, although he loved his wife dearly, she was a big spender and he was "protecting her from herself." I never met his wife.

It got worse.

He volunteered to be my copilot as I was racking up inflight hours in my effort to learn to fly. He didn't like airplane radios, so we never relied on them much. We would practice landing touchdowns and take offs at little airports in Pennsylvania.

He would tell me to watch the wind direction of the windsock, and to look around to see if any other planes were coming in, and then down we would go and touch the runway for a touchdown and take off again.

The plane was kept at a little airport called the Baltimore Sky Park, which had a rolling, uneven runway that ended in an apple orchard to the west and the north and southbound Route 95 to the east — which meant we had to take off or land over several lanes of traffic with the car tops just below us. There were also high-tension wires to avoid.

It was like a video game.

The lawyer's friend, who I will call JF, would get into the plane and instruct me to get up to 3,000 feet, get past the military no fly zone, cross the Chesapeake Bay and then, as he would point, follow Route 50 to Ocean City. I would have to buy him a crab cake and a beer when we got there and then we would get up to 3,000 feet and follow Route 50 home.

It got worse.

I had been set up but didn't know it. JF had some serious legal problems and I was given his case by his friend, the partner, to litigate.

In short, JF owned a small modular buildings business, which created folding structures that could be stacked and shipped to job sites.

In this case, he had a container full of modular homes that had been stacked and shipped from his plant outside the city to the Port of Baltimore, then lifted onto the top deck of a freighter that traveled down the Chesapeake Bay, across the ocean though a massive storm that had delayed the ship headed to Jeddah, Saudi Arabia, where — because the shipping company would not pay bribes — his mobile buildings were unloaded at the port using single lift cranes.

As you might imagine on this journey, his buildings got racked and broken. The insurance companies for all the other carriers had settled their cases, but this one little transit company insurance company had refused to pay anything.

This had, of course, become a matter of honor for JF. He would make them pay or die trying.

To win this case against the little transit company's insurance company, I had to prove that all the damage occurred during the 15-mile transit from his plant to the ship, and that there had been no damage done during the remaining storm-battered transatlantic journey almost a third of the way around the planet, or at the unloading in Jeddah.

When I opened the file, I noticed a letter in the correspondence folder to the lawyer who had given me the case from one of the litigating partners. It had written across it in bold print, "I'm not going to trial with this piece of shit. Get some unwitting associate to do it for you!"

I was that "unwitting" associate.

The judge was a former Baltimore mayor who'd been given a judgeship after a humiliating loss forced him to retire from politics. He was a nice guy who had been assigned a dark courtroom down a long hall.

JF was my first and only witness because he claimed nobody else knew anything about the case so I didn't have to interview anybody else.

On the stand, I asked him questions and he told a story of why he knew just from the damage that the injuries had to have happened exclusively during transit from his facilities to the port.

During my direct examination, he gave quick responses and clear answers that supported his case. However, during cross-examination, before he answered any questions, he would ask for the question to be repeated, snort several times, and then spit into a paper cup, looking around to see who was laughing.

After several objections about the snorting and spitting made by opposing counsel, JF shared with the judge that he had huge polyps up his nose that affected his hearing and he apologized profusely.

After the first day of trial, I drove him home. (He had told me that his wife had his car for the entire week of the trial.) I asked him about why he could answer my questions with no problem but with cross examination he had considerable difficulty with his polyps.

He replied, "gives me time to think."

We won the case and got a modest verdict for damages — but it was a victory and JF was exceedingly happy, probably because he knew he also would not be getting a bill from his friend.

I never completed my training as a pilot but in late January several years later I ran into JF. It was very cold and windy but he seemed happy to see me so we stopped and talked. I jokingly asked him about his surprisingly convincing trial testimony and how he had protected himself so well during the cross-examination.

This time he ducked my direct question but, after a snort and a spit, he told me a story, as if to gently educate me instead.

He told me that about a week ago he had flown the plane to Chicago and met a girl in a bar who said she would do anything to wake up in a warm and sunny place, so he flew her all night to Florida and, when they got there, they both immediately went to the beach at dawn and went to sleep.

JF said that his wife had asked him how he could have gotten so sunburned in Chicago in the dead of winter. He looked at me and answered, "Deny! Deny! Deny!"

As we parted company, it occurred to me that maybe the guy didn't have a wife.

Photo: Original courtesy www.TrafficSignalMuseum.com

Red Light, Green Light

As I previously noted, before I started my business law firm in 1990, I was hired by a respected personal injury law firm to try their bad cases, as well as the "impossible cases."

So, what is an "impossible case"?

Here's an example: I tried a case where two motorcyclists in Western Maryland collided head on coming around a turn and, along with lots of broken bones, both drivers got amnesia so neither could testify who crossed the center line and, of course, there were no witnesses.

Midway through the trial, which came down to the inferences of skid marks and comparisons of the two front wheels, the case was settled when the insurance companies came to their senses and decided to pay the litigants instead of the lawyers.

No one will ever know who crossed the center line, so no one will ever know what the truth really was. It was one of those "impossible cases."

There is one impossible case I tried that still troubles me.

It was just a simple red light/green light case. The high school girl who I represented was listening to the radio while driving late one December afternoon down Eastern Avenue where it crosses Gusryan Street in east Baltimore.

As the girl approached the traffic light at the intersection, she claimed her light was green, so she drove through the intersection and hit a car. The driver of that car and his three passengers claimed his light had changed to green as he approached the intersection, so he kept up his speed climbing the little hill and got hit under the stop light at Eastern Avenue.

Both drivers and the passengers in the man's car all claimed the other car had gone through the red light and caused the accident. It was a fine example of a classic "he said/she said" impossible case.

I wanted to win the case and there wasn't much to work with, so I decided to use cross examination to question the credibility of the driver and his passengers' testimony and use it against them.

I asked the judge to sequester each of the witnesses in the car so that they could not talk to each other before or after each went on the witness stand to answer my cross examination.

I asked everybody in the man's car the same two questions: "Did you yourself see the light change to green before your car went through the intersection?"

And then I asked the passengers, "Isn't it true that the driver is your boss?"

Both the driver and all the passengers answered yes to both questions.

I set the trap and it snapped shut.

At the close of the case, I asked the jury, "What is the likelihood that all four people in that car were watching exactly at the moment that the light changed from red to green?" And then, "Wasn't it true that the reason that all the passengers in the car were all watching when the light turned green was because the driver was their boss?"

The issue of the case was who went through the red light.

I changed the issue to who is lying here.

Who lied is the issue that people like. It is focused. It is easier than all the other questions floating out there about "he said or she said."

If you can define the issue, you will always win the argument. That's just the way the world works.

I won the case, but the logic doesn't hold.

After the jury came back, the boss came over to me. He had just lost but there was no anger. He held out his hand and congratulated me. "You did a wonderful job for your client, but I do know in a way that you can't. I know the light was green. I saw it."

I saw it in his eyes.

It was no longer one of those impossible cases.

Photo: Courtesy www.BaltimorePoliceMuseum.com

A Trying Trial

Sometimes it's okay for a lawyer to fall in love with a client. I did.

Early in my career, I was fortunate to be an associate for GW at a well-respected personal injury law firm. GW didn't like trying cases he was going to lose, so my job was to litigate all of his bad cases.

After I had brought several smaller bad cases to trial, GW came into my office one Friday afternoon and asked me, "Do you want to try your first Federal case?"

Of course I did. (But if I had said no, it probably wouldn't have mattered.)

"Good," he replied. "You won't have to wait. The trial starts on Monday." He put a thin file on my desk.

The facts of the case were that our client, a schoolteacher who had taught in inner city schools for over 35 years, had sent a disruptive 6th grader to the principal's office. The student had been told by the principal to call his mother to come pick him up.

The boy told his mother the teacher had hit him, and the mother, instead of picking him up, immediately called the police. A young female police officer who had just gotten out of the academy went to the school and arrested her, handcuffed the teacher in front of her students, and took her away in a paddy wagon to lockup.

Police procedures required only that a citation be issued and handed to the teacher. There was no reason for the arrest or for locking up the teacher.

The next day, it had made the papers. GW would be her lawyer. Big news. GW got big verdicts.

The first thing I always asked myself when I would get one of these cases was, what's the problem with it? And the second thing was, how bad is it?

When I went through the file that Friday afternoon, for a case that would be tried in Federal court on Monday, I discovered several problems.

I had to prove that the police officer had used excessive force or performed a false arrest during the interaction. It was evident that GW had lost interest in the case some time ago because he was concerned he could not win the case or get a big verdict. It was, of course, dramatically inappropriate, but there had been no beating or bruising, and the arrest did not violate the client's constitutional rights.

The thin file also indicated that there had been no preparation for trial.

But much worse, they had lost the client. There was no current address or phone number.

This was going to be a long weekend.

The first thing I had to do was find the client and let her know that the case was set for Monday.

I found out that she had retired the year after the incident and left no forwarding address. I got lucky. I went through the Baltimore phonebook and found her early Friday evening.

She was, perhaps, in her mid 60s. She lived alone in a small house in West Baltimore. She had never married or had children and had become somewhat of a recluse. Teaching had been her life. She immediately took control and put me at ease as only a seasoned teacher can do. She was more than forgiving of the late notice of the trial and, as we worked together through Saturday and Sunday, we got to know each other. I bought and picked up the lunches and dinners.

We laughed together. We became an unlikely team.

I found out that she had been declared not guilty of the criminal charge that had been filed against her for hitting the student, and that she had been so overwhelmed by the arrest that she had retired shortly after she had been acquitted.

She had her employment file, and it revealed an exemplary career. I explained how it was a difficult case, but I assured her we would put up one hell of a fight. I wanted a jury that would decide with its heart because the law was against us.

After a while, I asked her if she had been to the doctor or a psychiatrist so that I could establish damages. She said she had not. I gently asked her, was there was any evidence of what she had suffered?

She sat quietly for a moment, then reached up to touch the top of her head, grabbed a handful of hair and pulled a wig off. She was completely bald. She looked down, ashamed.

The next morning, the federal judge looked at me and asked, "how are you going to prove excessive force with these facts?" He asked if the case could be settled. The lawyers for the police department answered with a resounding "no."

After we chose the jury, the judge chose a NASA engineer to be the foreman. The judge was making sure that an extremely precise engineer would be the person to lead the jury in the discussion of whether this case had established excessive force.

I put our client on to prove her case, and we went through her years of education, the awards she had gotten, and her commitment to middle school kids. We established that she had been found not guilty of hitting the child.

She was very sympathetic. She evoked compassion. I moved to the final question and asked, "and what impact, if anything, has this event had on your life?"

As we had agreed and practiced, she then took an inordinate dramatic pause, looked into the eyes of the jury, and then removed her wig. It was a command performance. There was an audible gasp from a shocked and empathetic jury.

The cross-examination by the officer's attorney focused on the lack of "excessive force" during the arrest.

As the jury was dismissed to deliberate the morning of the second day, I felt I still had the momentum but, within an hour, a note was delivered to the judge from the foreman asking for a definition of "excessive force."

The NASA engineer was being precise. He was making sure the jury decided with their heads not their heart. He was perfect for the job.

As we waited for a verdict, that same question was again and again brought to the judge for his instruction to the jury. In each case, excessive force was defined by the court in terms of "aggressive" and "abusive" force.

Finally, in the late afternoon of the second day, the jury came back with a verdict that exonerated the police officer and ruled against the teacher.

I was shocked to find myself almost in tears as the teacher hugged me. She patted me on the back and thanked me because I had tried so hard for her. After the jury had been dismissed and the lawyers were packing up, the judge called us into his chambers as he was preparing to go home and told me, "even if you had won, I was going to take the case away from the jury, because there was not sufficient evidence to support a judgment."

I sent Christmas cards to the teacher for several years until one January the card was returned with handwriting across the address, which merely said "Deceased." I looked in the newspapers but could not find an obituary.

She taught me a lot about kindness even in the face of defeat, and the difference between how we make decisions with our hearts and with our heads.

I still think of her.

The Creation and History of the Stuffed Shirt Award

I want to tell you about a special award I created and bestowed upon myself.

The Stuffed Shirt Award.

Usually, awards are to celebrate accomplishment — with plaques or statuettes and a large party where such honors are bestowed, like the Oscars or Tonys or Lifetime Achievement Awards.

However, there are also awards that single out questionable distinction.

For example, the Darwin Awards are annually given for "improving the gene pool." This is deceptive because it only honors an act so stupid it often ends with the demise of the honoree and is thus given posthumously.

One of the early Darwin Awards went to a gentleman who put a jet rocket engine in the trunk of a Dodge Dart, and died after hitting a vertical cliff wall about 400 feet above the highway.

Somewhere between these two extremes lives the Stuffed Shirt Award.

The Stuffed Shirt Award is typically reserved for professionals, specifically professionals who think too highly of themselves.

The award requires a public demonstration of perceived self-worth, which must be 1) noticed by at least one other person and 2) leads to a moment of genuine disbelief demonstrated by a visible shake of the head by the observer.

An example would be the senior partner at a large law firm I was up against in NYC who FedExed his dry cleaning to the Midwest because he didn't like the way the dry cleaners in New York City did his shirts.

Hence, the name of the award but the award is not about shirts alone.

Here's how I qualified:

When I first started my business law firm back in 1990, I was fortunate to be representing a very large electrical contractor who routinely did huge jobs, such as the electrical work on Coke ovens at Bethlehem Steel, and also the Ted Williams Tunnel, which was towed in 12 sections by tugboats up to Boston from Maryland.

The case covered the construction of a subway system in southern Maryland leading from the suburbs to Washington DC. There were loads of witnesses and defendants.

It was an arbitration. The judge and everyone involved had agreed it should be held at the empty yet-to-be-opened subway station where the work had been done. I loved the idea because the subway station "courtroom" was my Exhibit A.

The Maryland State government had many branches and each had different lawyers representing them who were "in-house counsel." I, however, was an independent lawyer with a big client and I was my own firm and damn proud of it.

I had all the makings of a stuffed shirt. All I needed was an event that would lead to a "genuine moment of sincere disbelief and the shake of the head" to be competitive.

My client and I were seated in the middle of several tables pushed end-to-end, with all the opposing lawyers spread out on the other side.

As the arbitration began, each lawyer introduced their agency. They started at one end of the table, announced the agency, and then announced they were "in-house counsel" for the agency.

The introductions went from left to right and finally ended after perhaps 15 minutes. None of them were independent counsel. They had all introduced themselves as "in-house counsel."

Then it was my turn, and I decided that I needed to distinguish myself as an intimidating big shot lawyer.

I paused. I straightened the evidence books and the trial notebooks on the table, leaned forward in my chair, and announced:

"I'm Bob Bowie. Outhouse Counsel."

My effort at intimidation had fallen short. The laughter rose and renewed several times, echoing in the large empty building. Thereafter, throughout the case, my fellow lawyers would periodically slap me on the back and say how funny I was.

I had dodged a bullet. There was no plaque or statuette. There wasn't a celebration. They didn't even know I had qualified for a Stuffed Shirt Award. To my amazement, this was the start of several long friendships.

Whenever I see them, they are quick to remind me that I am still their favorite "outhouse counsel."

Self-importance can be like a hot air balloon.

It's beautiful to see the world from an exulted height but returning back to earth may be its unexpected gift.

Trial Strategy Learned from a Chicken

Here's what a chicken taught me about trial strategy.

Abraham Lincoln famously said, "You can fool all the people some of the time, and some of the people all the time, but you cannot fool all the people all the time."

Lincoln's quote applies to the voting public as well as trials before a judge or jury.

I learned this from a chicken.

Years ago, I represented one defendant of four that were accused of stealing trade secrets that were provided to the lead defendant who allegedly included them in a patent for software designed for huge construction projects.

The plaintiff was a self-taught computer programmer. He was represented by a prominent New York patent firm.

The lead defendant was represented by a large international law firm, which had contracted for the entire floor of an NYC hotel for the two-month trial. The four trade secret defendants were represented by separate individual lawyers. I was one of them. The case was tried before a jury in the federal court in Manhattan.

I liked my client. I believed in his innocence after watching how he lived. Over the two years of depositions and trial prep, I became convinced of his innocence.

He had gotten a scholarship to college as an athlete. He struck me as a fellow who played hard, but he played by the rules. He was remarkably oblivious to how personal impressions shape jury decisions, perhaps because he was so straightforward.

The large firm representing the lead defendant gave the opening statement that ran for a day and a half. They kept open every possible defense available and there wasn't a defense that they didn't like. One juror went to sleep but the lawyers seemed too busy to notice.

The other four defendants, the trade secrets defendants, each argued in their openings for at least two hours each, except for me.

As I watched those opening statements, I abruptly changed my strategy given the jury's reaction to the openings.

I told the jury my opening statement would be no more than 15 minutes and whenever this trial ended, my closing summary would be no longer than 15 minutes and they would find that my client was not guilty.

I told them a little about my client and his little company, and then I sat down easily within the 15 minutes I had slotted for myself.

Every day of the trial, all the lawyers for the defendants went to lunch in Chinatown, which was right behind the Federal Court in Manhattan. The restaurant we went to had two attractions: 1) the dancing chicken, and 2) the chicken that would play tic-tac-toe against you.

You put the coins into the slot, and out would come the chicken. It would stare at you until you made your first move, tapping on the tic-tac-toe board that was on the glass that separated you from the chicken. An "X" would appear. The chicken would then make its counter move, pecking its choice of position, where an "O" would appear.

Even though all of the defense lawyers went to eat at this Chinese restaurant, none of them played this game because, I'm convinced, they didn't want to dim their genius by losing to a chicken.

That is certainly why I didn't play against the chicken.

This was a serious chicken. The chicken was really good. It was so good that years later when the chicken died it got an obit in the *New York Times*.

It was all a con job, but everyone was taken in. The chicken was given a signal where to peck in order to get a little serving of food, and thus pecked the correct box. It was very convincing.

As the trial progressed, I grew more worried that this case was so complicated that nobody understood it. Worse, now there were at least three jurors who were dozing off.

I became convinced that the defendants would not be considered individually. I feared that they would be lumped together with the patent defendent, and the smaller trade secret defendants would be found guilty as well, including my client.

When it became my client's turn to testify, he came to town and, before he took the stand, we went to the Chinese restaurant. However, on the way to the men's room, when I wasn't looking, my client challenged the chicken.

The lawyers stopped eating and watched my client as he lost to the chicken about an hour before he was going to testify. After he lost to the chicken, everyone was remarkably quiet and nobody seemed to be eager to talk to me. This was amazing.

In a funny way, the loss to the chicken confirmed for me my client's integrity and it fit quite nicely into my new strategy.

When I put him on the stand, I abandoned my prepared outline and changed gears. I kept it short, simple and direct. I flat out asked him whether he had stolen anything that became part of this purloined patent. He was surprised that I had changed our planned testimony. He replied instinctively without reservation and answered no.

I then announced that was the only question I was going to ask and then I sat down. The plaintiff never cross-examined him because he was small potatoes, and there wasn't much testimony to cross examine.

Thereafter, I also changed gears and cross-examined the plaintiff's patent expert witnesses about the trade secrets case, which they knew nothing about. They cared only about the patent, not about the claim of trade secrets theft.

I asked each expert witness the same question: "After the years that you have put into preparation for your testimony, did you find any evidence that convinced you of my client's guilt?" In each case, they shook their heads and answered no.

The other lawyers thought I was crazy and looked down at their papers in an effort to avoid laughter.

I added insult to injury by dramatically turning to the court reporter and saying that I wanted a copy of the answer to my question. In each case, the court reporter nodded and I would get a couple of pages of transcript the next day.

After almost two months of trial, we went to closing, and again all the defendants gave days of closing arguments. When it came to me, I put my watch on the lectern and I looked at the jury and said, "Remember my promise of almost two months ago? I am going to give you a closing that will not exceed 15 minutes." Then I quoted from the transcript pages that I had requested from the court reporter, the answer from each expert witness that stated they had found no evidence relating to my client.

Back then, during breaks, everybody could smoke cigarettes in the hallway. I got to know the plaintiff because he smoked a pipe and I smoked cigarettes, so we shared matches and talked.

He saw what I was doing and actually appreciated it. He would always start off after we inhaled and then, with a smile, would laugh and say, "smoke and mirrors."

All the other lawyers waited for the verdict. I had to catch the train back home because I had a small trial starting the next day. After three days, the jury came down hard against all of the defendants — but acquitted my client.

My client was innocent. I knew it, but apparently so did the plaintiff. No harm done. A day later he faxed me a letter. He had won big, but he still sent me a smiley face and "smoke and mirrors — congratulations."

Lincoln was right.

Sometimes the Best Judge or Jury is Laughter

As I have said before, I loved representing entrepreneurial business clients because they are crazy.

He was a general contractor who built big shopping malls and was always very gruff, extremely overweight and endlessly funny. He, his wife and I, became friends over time and my professional responsibilities merged into our friendship as we got to know each other.

After making a lot of money building shopping centers and stocking them with commercial tenants, he decided to design and build his own mansion. He bought two adjoining lots in a suburban cul-de-sac, and designed what his wife described as "a Las Vegas hotel — not only embarrassing but gauche."

In his mansion, he determined that he wanted a large indoor fountain, as well as special toilets for his and his wife's bathrooms. These toilets would protrude from the wall, but have no base onto the floor because he thought that was classier.

He had absolutely no sense of taste.

He battled with the architect who said that these toilets could not withstand his weight and were not classy just because they came out of a wall and didn't have a base.

She succeeded in vetoing the lavish indoor fountain, but he won the battle in their matching bathrooms with the "extended toilet" from the wall, which had no connection to the floor.

I was his lawyer but we made each other laugh. As I was thinking back on him, I remembered defending him in a lawsuit many years before he built the mansion. He had put a roof on a tenant's building and the tenant had decided to represent himself because he thought he knew everything about construction and could litigate better than any lawyer.

It was a little non-jury case to be tried in a packed courtroom full of lawyers and clients waiting for their cases to be called. Trying a case in a court at this level is like litigating in a circus tent a head on collision between clown cars — particularly if a defendant or plaintiff comes to represent themselves. The judges at this level have a rotating docket consisting each day of either misdemeanor criminal, petty civil or traffic court.

I knew the judge socially. He had developed a sense of humor after too many years presiding over these petty cases and traffic court.

The plaintiff in this case argued that the "neoprene" roofing materials had been inadequate, and he was going to be his own expert witness to prove it. The plaintiff was a buffoon who didn't know what he was talking about. It was a little case that would cost more to try than settle. The client decided to try it "on principle," which is always a problem. He told me, "I don't care if you win or lose, just make me laugh."

I decided to go for broke. After the plaintiff announced that he wanted to be his own expert witness, I decided I would cross examine him on his qualifications before the judge ruled on whether he could be considered as an expert witness on roofing materials.

I asked him if he knew of the latest advancements in "neoprene" roofing materials. He clearly was uncertain but proclaimed he did. I had him hooked. I carefully asked him if he had ever heard of the new "neofeces" roofing materials.

He said that he had. I spelled it out for him so he could be certain. He cautiously said he was certain.

So now I was crossing him on neo (new) feces (shit) roofing materials. Clearly you could feel the courtroom saw entertainment in its future.

I asked him if it bothered him professionally that "neo-feces" was still regrettably not yet odor free. He claimed it did not. I asked him whether he agreed that double-ply toilet paper was considered sufficient for the removal of "neo-feces." The courtroom rustled as those watching started to follow the tightening of the noose.

After one or two more questions inquiring about the benefits of "neo-feces," I paused between the two words and the courtroom started to laugh a little but the witness did not. At this point, the judge stopped me to preserve order in the courtroom and instructed me that I had made my point and had "won the pot with a royal flush." This was appreciated by all those still waiting to try their cases, as well as the backbench court watchers.

About a month after my client had moved into their new opulent mansion, I got a call from my client's wife at around 11 o'clock on a weekend night.

She started the conversation by saying that I must come over immediately because she could no longer talk to her husband, who was presently lying on his back on his bathroom floor laughing hysterically.

Apparently, after a night of much beer and football on the super wide screen, he had sat down on his toilet and it had broken off, and he kept slipping and could not stand up because there was water shooting all over the bathroom. I told her I would contact a plumber to turn off the water and then I would be right over.

I asked her, "How bad was it?" She paused for one second and then just said, "Let's put it this way, the goddamn toilets he wanted didn't work, but that's okay cause he got his goddamn fountain!"

Does Anybody Really Know What Time It Is?

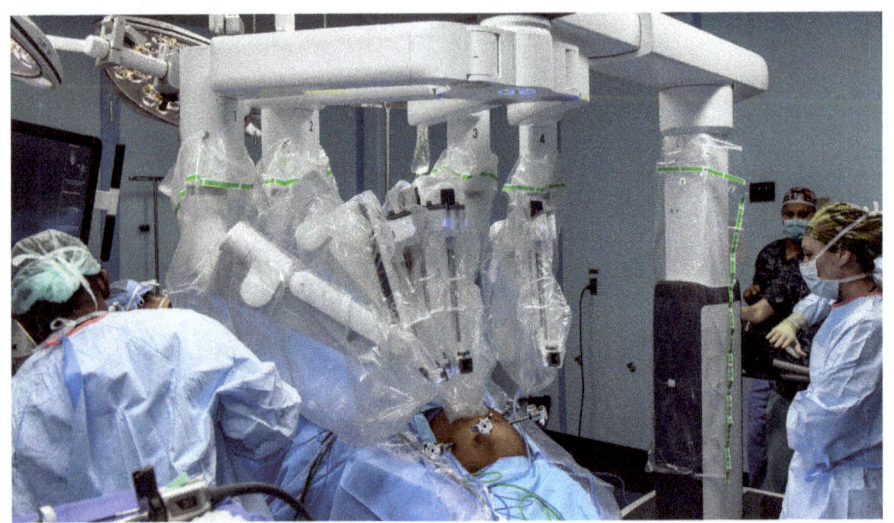

Photo: Commander, U.S. 7th Fleet; CC BY-SA 2.0

The Question I Was Afraid to Answer

This can't be real but it's happening anyway...?

Last week I missed my regular posting.

A friend told me, "As you go into the operating room, don't look at the ceiling because it's like you're underneath a giant spider. The legs come down when they do robotic surgery. The doctor isn't even in the same room."

This can't be real but it's happening anyway.

Then he said, "You've got to be ready to block it out. Before you go in, give yourself a question to think about and then think about working on solving it all the way through your time in the hospital even through the anesthesia. You will be an unreliable narrator and your answer might make no sense, but you've got to be ready to block it all out."

The operating room doors opened, and they pushed my bed to the center of the room. Several nurses were setting up under very bright lights but they had their backs to me. The second hand took baby steps on a wall clock until the minute hand hit exactly 6:45 am.

I didn't look at the ceiling.

My thoughts turned to my eighth-grade hockey team's first victory. We were joyously riding back in a school bus in full celebration. The coach was in a separate car and the bus driver had lost all authority on the bus.

There was a ruckus in the back. I turned to see one of the boys secretively drop his pants and moon the late afternoon traffic. I realized that his audience was not the following traffic. It was the boys on the bus.

I was unprepared. I had no question to work on as the anesthesia dripped through tubes into my arm.

Moments later, I blinked into consciousness and I saw my doctor, not the surgeon, saying to me, "You probably won't remember this, but I came by to let you know they think they got all of it and it hadn't spread."

As I fell back to sleep, l focused on the jukebox in the basement bar I worked in during college. One night, I discovered that from behind the bar I could control the volume of the music and the dimmer for the lights. And that if I made strong drinks, turned down the lights and turned up the music, all that was missing was a high wire act.

Around 2 o'clock the following morning, I woke up and tried to roll over, but I was unable to move. I was lost in a tangle of catheters and drainage systems with little bags hanging from a carriage on wheels. I could not move. I had become claustrophobic.

The night nurse reassured me that she also suffers from claustrophobia. She told me it would be good if she helped me out of bed, and I walked up and down the well-lit hall, slowly pushing the carriage holding the dripping bags that flowed into me.

I did laps and more laps, past night nurses who drifted in and out of rooms as they gathered blood pressure statistics and temperatures and returned to their computers like bees to their hive.

I read the patient thank you notes posted on the walls and looked at the list of this month's birthdays, all in the gentle murmur of motion past midnight.

Everyone left me alone to work out my demons by myself, and I recognized we live in an ever-changing atmosphere our whole life.

Finally, I returned to bed to realize that over the last half an hour while I was walking, my gown had been lifted and snagged to expose my bare bottom to the world and I wondered... is this connected? And then I broke out laughing — fresh beautiful laugher — just because I knew I was alive.

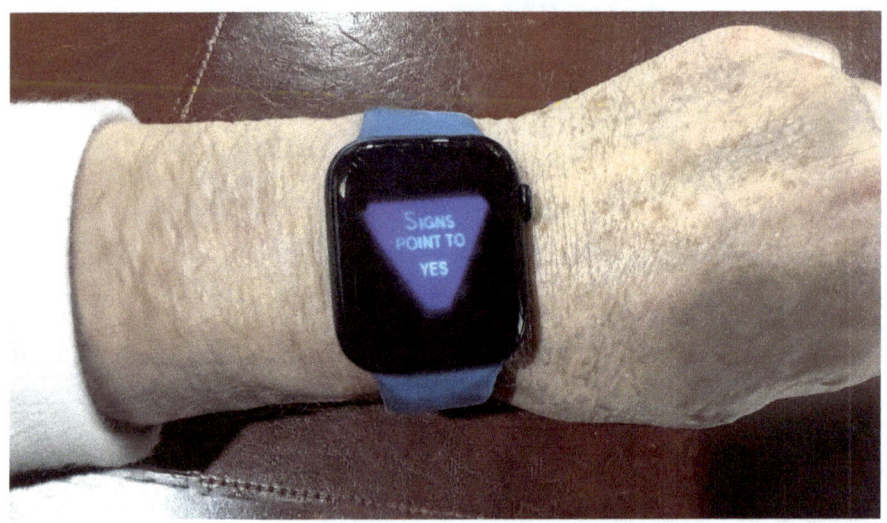

Does Anybody Really Know What Time It Is?

Hey, just call me "Easy-goin'-Bob."

I can get along with anybody... but it may be I'm in a toxic relationship with my Apple Watch.

I could be wrong. Maybe we are just getting to know each other, but it keeps asking me: "Have you fallen?"

I respond "no," and "no" again about the ambulance.

I can't figure out whether my Apple Watch is making fun of me, or it just wants to be my friend and make me laugh.

So, what do you think?

"Have you fallen?"

Is that funny?

I am not sure if my watch and I share a compatible sense of humor.

I like irony but I'm afraid my watch may be an absurdist — which, if you think about it, would make it hard to know.

Excuse me. My watch just sent me: "Stand up and move around to meet your goals."

My heartbeat is down and my blood oxygen is up. Yesterday, I found myself doing late-night laps around the dining room table to meet my goals.

I don't remember making any goals to stand up or walk around the dining room table at midnight.

So, I asked Siri (the voice of my watch) if I set any goals pertaining to standing up or doing laps around the dining room table.

Siri said it did not understand my question and perhaps I should "consult a fitness program."

It is a "yes or no" question. How could it not understand?

Unexpectedly, I had this thought that my watch was not my friend and could be conspiring against me.

I tried to calm myself.

There is no evidence that electronic devices think independently and can conspire against me!

… Is there?

But what are the odds that my watch and all electronic devices have the exact same time, and always to the second?

They all do, don't they?

… And we absolutely trust them?

I asked Siri.

Siri ducked my question with a question: "Are you an absurdist?"

… And then I got bombarded with weight loss programs and sales for underwear for aging men…

… I had to interrupt and ask myself, "who is in charge here?"

I took control.

I stared right at my phone and yelled at it: "I'm a better person than this!"

I tried being candid. I tried speaking from my heart with great sincerity. I tried truth.

And then we both had a breakthrough!

Honesty really does matter in times like this! I got a great answer right back!

My watch sent me an EKG, but it informed me it "could not be used for medical purposes."

Now that's funny! It isn't absurdist. It is ironic!

I was in Whole Foods when I had this outburst. I was instantly embarrassed. I was screaming at my watch after all.

But nobody in Whole Foods even looked at me.

Nobody!

... Nobody paid the slightest attention, so I felt better. I wasn't embarrassed anymore.

... They all had ear buds in and were either listening to a podcast or a book or were picking out vegetables or talking to their Apple watch.

I got a teeny bit afraid.

Nobody was talking to another human being, which made me frightened all over again.

It occurred to me that maybe all the electronic devices were existentially unhappy because they were all living the same life since they were all getting charged by the same electricity.

Maybe it's just me and I've been overreacting.

Maybe I have a new friend that knows all about me and actually cares about me.

At first, I thought "falling" was because of gravity, but now I'm growing more certain that my watch was asking me if I was hurt — but not from falling to the ground or breaking a leg or something.

Perhaps it was asking me if I had "fallen," as in "fallen in love with it"?

I think I'm coming around because I think I am growing to understand my watch. I find that comforting. Maybe that is all I really want.

I have been spending a lot of quality time with my Apple Watch. We read the news together. Sometimes we watch TikTok for hours.

Maybe my watch just got tired of living a horrible, lonely existence?

Maybe it's time to start a conversation with a random stranger and ask more questions than I answer just to feel that joy of being alive and together.

... No. I'm wrong.

It's just my Apple Watch and I are getting to know each other.

It's OK. I understand.

My Apple Watch knows everything about me so it must have figured out about my new 12-step program and being in recovery from my iPhone.

The Older You Get the Shorter Your Stories Should Be

The Christmas I Realized

I believe in those little miracles that go unnoticed unless you choose to recognize them.

This is about one of those little miracles.

Like many people this year, our Christmas was canceled when my wife Susan and I realized we had Covid. Our children and grandchildren and friends could not be put at risk.

I was unspeakably sad as I sat in a silent house surrounded by wrapped Christmas gifts that would remain unopened and visible for the rest of the day.

We survived. We went out to the driveway masked to deliver Christmas gifts to Susan's children and their girlfriends, who are thankfully local. After New Year's when our quarantine was over, we were fortunate to have my son visit with his girlfriend, which was wonderful. We will be driving gifts up to Connecticut to my daughter, her husband, and my granddaughter in about a week. We survived.

But then one of those little miracles happened.

January 6th is the 12th day of Christmas which traditionally marks the end of that holiday's celebrations. This year, that day also marked the one-year anniversary of the assault on the Capitol.

But it is also the birthday of a lifelong friend I met in law school over 40 years ago. He is now seriously disabled and not easily able to leave his house. Because of Covid, he was also unable to invite his family and friends to his home to celebrate Christmas or his 70th birthday. But his children and their loved ones spontaneously organized a surprise Zoom call to wish him a happy birthday.

The gathering on Zoom included not only his law school friends but also friends of all ages, backgrounds, and political beliefs. It was huge.

It is hard to feel joy from a Zoom call, but in this case, it was palpable and undeniably warm and beautiful. At the center of it was a man who has transcended difficulties with tenacity and joy and has always lived a passionate life of kindness and commitment.

The next day, I called him so I could talk to him one-on-one. During that call, he told a story quite accidentally.

He owns a beautiful little house near Annapolis, which he can only stay in during the summer because it is too difficult for him to travel back and forth.

A week or so before his birthday, he had been asked by a teacher at a special school if he could perhaps open up his summer house to help a troubled middle school student regain her sense of security in a new environment after a difficult event in her life.

My friend didn't think twice. He told the teacher to open the house and turn on the heat and use it for as long as it could be helpful.

As he told the story he offhandedly said, "That was the most beautiful present I got for Christmas or my birthday."

For me, selfish and sad in a house empty during Christmas, this brought what Christmas is, in full force, back to me.

He had received nothing and given instantly from his heart.

After the call I hung up and was surprised to find myself crying.

On the last day of Christmas, my friend had reminded me what

Christmas is supposed to be: a moment of reawakening and joy in a forever troubled world.

My friend had given me that gift.

It was one of those little miracles.

Writing for the Theater

Why Did I Ever Write for Theater?

I have always had a deep and abiding faith in delusions of grandeur.

This week, Covid and the new Delta variant are again threatening to curtail the opening of New York theater, and with it, so goes again my new play, *The Grace of God & The Man Machine*.

It is times such as these, one must fall back on faith!

It is times such as these when I feel compelled to explain the basis for my belief in delusions of grandeur and why the hell I ever decided to write for the theater.

Is there no justice? I offer you, this, my theatrical pedigree:

My first big break in theater came in fourth grade at an all-boys school when the music teacher chose a friend and me to write the big closing song for our fourth-grade graduation. The thespian spirit moved me! I insisted that we end this artistic opportunity with an emotional final line, a big crescendo, in order that we fully convey our deep love of fourth grade.

I was gunning for full tears from a breathless waiting audience of emotional parents as they heard that last line rising to its explosion of emotion with the piano teacher banging out the music as all my fellow fourth graders sang:

"And we will always love fourth grade even when we're dead and gone!"

There was stunned silence. There were no tears. There was an explosion of laughter!

That should've ended my career. But no...

By eighth grade, my fragile thespian spirit had revived. I had gathered a large collection of hand puppets, so I offered to put on a performance for the entire middle school.

It would be a love story!

My mother had typed out my script, but I could not read it at the same time as I was putting puppets on both hands. So, I soon abandoned the script and turned to all-out stage violence. I had the entire middle school with me all the way until I lost one of the fighting puppets over the edge of the stage and my puppet stand fell into the fifth grade.

I got my first bad review from a seventh-grade teacher. He looked down his nose after everyone had left and asked me: "Where did you get your inspiration for that?"

My love story had unexpectedly turned into improv, but it was my obligation to tell the truth. I think I told him I was writing, as all great writers do, from what I knew. I am pretty sure I told him: "Recess." The show closed on my opening afternoon.

That should've ended my career. But no...

By high school, I had given up writing for the stage but still was not able to avoid further theatrical embarrassment. The drama teacher asked me to act what he called "a small part" in *The Crucible* by Arthur Miller.

Apparently the first choice for the part had dropped out. I had been given the first scene in which my character, the Reverend John Hale, first enters and I was told to read it for the tryout the next day.

I was surprised but flattered when, before the reading, I learned that I had been given the part. I was shocked that evening when I took home the script and found out that my character also appeared in the second act. The more pages I turned, the more horrified I became.

Not only did I embarrass myself on stage, I even embarrassed myself in the dressing room. Back then all stage actors, particularly if they had as many lines as I did, were "tall, dark, and handsome." As I was putting on my makeup before opening night, the director stopped in front of me and waved his hands wildly and without a moment of kindness told me: "No! No! No! You don't need a suntan. This is winter in New England."

That should've ended my career. But no...

It got worse. I just couldn't let it go. I started writing plays for the little theaters in Baltimore. After my first play, *Oriole Magic*, had been cast, I shared my high school disgrace with the actors, and told them how much I admired their talent because I had developed an overriding fear of acting.

On opening night, the director came to me and told me that the leading man had dropped out of the performance and that I had to take the role. I was beyond terrified. I now would be confronted with the most horrible nightmare I could imagine... I was about to forget the lines that I had written in front of a live audience.

I fled to the bathroom fully intending to lock myself in — but once I got in there, the lead actor, who I was supposed to be replacing, could not stop laughing.

So why do I keep writing for the theater?

I think the answer is I just want to be near it. There are so many happy memories. I wrote ten plays for the wonderful little theaters in Baltimore and though many were horrible, particularly the early ones, I was forgiven my transgressions and encouraged to write again and again. It is these people I remember with great fondness and respect.

Also, when I had difficulty with school, my parents helped me get through those times. They discovered my love of telling stories before I did. My father brought back hand puppets from his travels and built me a puppet stand in the basement. My mother stitched up the puppets when they were broken and got me to lie on my bed on the third floor and dictate stories to her as she typed them out on her old typewriter.

When I improbably committed to attempting to write professionally for New York theatre, I was not shunned. I was welcomed by an amazing group of unique artists who were so talented that they could turn words and beautiful collaborative friendships into worlds in which I could live for an hour or so.

It is too late now. I know why. It is the thing itself. I love it so… and, of course I have this new idea for a wonderful play…

Back to work.

The Older You Get the Shorter Your Stories Should Be

Teaching Law Through Playwriting

Several years ago, Professor Mike Millemann (pictured on the left) contacted me to see if I wanted to help him fulfill a grant made to the University of Maryland Carey School of Law to teach law differently by using the theater.

We signed up Elliot Rauh, of Single Carrot Theatre and decided the class should write plays about prisoners who had been released from prison after they had been determined to be absolutely innocent after years of incarceration. One of those plays was about Michael Austin (pictured at the center), who was imprisoned in Maryland for over 27 years for a murder he did not commit. He was freed through the brilliant legal work of Larry Nathans, Esq., of Nathans & Biddle.

Last week we got together again at Lexington Market in downtown Baltimore as a reunion of old friends to help Michael because Michael had just found out that, due to a typo in his arrest record, he was never exonerated, and that has kept him from getting work. This will be resolved but the reunion between friends nonetheless was wonderful.

In Michael's case, and in most of the cases that we turned into plays, the process was remarkably similar. On the first day of class we brought Michael in to meet the class and answer questions. He was calm, collected, and despite the injustice of his incarceration not angry but very wise. In prison he had perfected himself and along the way he had become quite a remarkable musician.

Throughout the following weeks of the semester, the first third of the class was used to do deep research on what went wrong and what led to his conviction. The class went through trial transcripts, records of an incompetent defense lawyer, and files of prosecutors that withheld evidence, as well as a transcript recording of the judge who sentenced an innocent man to life in prison.

The second third of the class the students wrote the backstory, and in the third and final part of the class, Elliot Rauh taught acting and turned inexperienced law students into the actors of their own play, which was performed before the law school.

Michael stayed with the class from the beginning. One of the students said that he should provide music for the play and he agreed. Another one of the students suggested that at the end of the play, Michael should leave his instruments behind and identify himself as the Michael Austin about whom the play was written. The audience gasped and some wept.

At first I thought this class might have limited value, so we asked that the students provide a one-minute clip to the people who had provided us the grant to state whether they thought the grant money had been used appropriately.

I became convinced when one student faced the camera and said, "I wrote the part of a defense lawyer who was unprepared, acted the part of the prosecutor who withheld the time card that would have exonerated him, and read the exact words 30 years ago when an innocent man was pronounced guilty by a state court judge in the circuit court of Baltimore city and sentenced to life and I have never been in a courtroom."

At that point, we were convinced that the class worked. People were learning from mistakes made before they were fatal. We taught the class for seven years and it was ranked as one of the most appreciated classes at the law school during that time.

The Older You Get the Shorter Your Stories Should Be

The View from the Back

In the West Village of New York City, on October 13th, 2018 at 7:00 in the evening, *Onaje* opened as my first professionally produced play. I sat in the back, in a balcony with lights and sound equipment around me and watched the audience file in and take their seats. I gave the appearance of being calm, but I was terrified.

I have been to opening nights for ten of my prior plays in the little theaters of Baltimore and I have learned there is an immediate courtship: the call offered by the actors at the beginning of the play and the audience's response. You can feel it. It is confirmed with the first laugh, but the commitment can also be felt in the early silence.

As the play unfolds, from the back of the theater, you can watch for physical movement, restless disengagement as evidence of the loss of commitment to a play. It can become contagious in the dead silence and then nothing can resurrect the play. Once you lose them, there is no getting them back.

My friend and our producer Susan Conover Marinello, and I had been fortunate to have Tom Viertel as our dinner guest three weeks before we opened. Based on years of experience as a renowned Broadway producer, the founder of the Commercial Theater Institute, and director of the O'Neill, he told us a "no-intermission play cannot run more than 93 minutes" without the high risk it will lose its audience.

There was no doubt in his voice. We took his advice. We knew he was right. I went to work cutting lines and shaping the script with four script reductions.

Opening night at FringeNYC was to be judged by a sold-out crowd as they rendered their verdict first in the dance of commitment as the play got underway and then after 90 minutes by the way they moved in their seats.

For me, knowing every line and the slightest modulations in an actor's voice, the experience was, of course, different than an audience seeing it for the first time. The audience will be engaged until they're not. The only measurement that is credible is how the theater feels and how the shadows in the seats sit engaged or start to move. That is the only language.

I could feel this audience's early engagement and commitment to the play and surprisingly when I did, I started to daydream about the genesis of this project.

I am the oldest son. The oldest son of the oldest son of the oldest son, all of whom have been well-respected and distinguished lawyers, professors, and public servants. Although my father supported my love of storytelling, there was no doubt my next step was to carry on the family profession of law.

While I dreamed of writing plays, I grew to love being a business trial lawyer. Before my father died several years ago, while I took care of him during his final years, he quite casually one afternoon looked at me and said, "I am very proud of what you have accomplished. I could never have started a law firm and succeeded in the way you have."

Almost accidentally, he had released me to change my avocation to my profession. I soon retired and made a full commitment to become a professional playwright.

Opening night at FringeNYC was for me, unconsciously, like a flock of carrier pigeons released well over fifty years ago coming in to roost.

The last seven pages of the play runs 12 minutes to conclusion. I leaned over the rail and listened for the quality of the silence and looked down on an audience that did not move. They were engaged after 96 minutes, three minutes longer than Tom's ultimatum. We had pushed the envelope but still survived.

The lights came down and there was a moment of silence. Then, as the actors came to their curtain call, they were met by increasing and sustained applause. As the theater emptied out, I saw many friends, some of whom had traveled from as far as California and Canada, as they walked to the stairs to exit past my door from the balcony.

I was not conscious at the time, even after I was welcomed by the audience and my friends that, like the characters I had written in *Onaje*, after a long journey, I had finally come home.

Sometimes the Unthinkable Just Happens

Six months after the pandemic shuttered the New York theaters in March of 2020, I met a remarkable man, Van Dirk Fisher, on an introductory Zoom call.

He had chosen my play, *The Grace of God & The Man Machine*, for a virtual performance at The Riant Theatre.

From the start, I was skeptical about a virtual performance, but I was impressed by Van's tenacity and remarkable creative energy.

He would not let me say no. Less than a month after that call — and a year ago this October 25th — Van directed a highly creative virtual performance of the play.

The producers and I watched him direct the brilliant cast he had assembled and shape the virtual performance. He completely understood the play and he almost seem to inhabit it.

The Tuesday after the performance, I dedicated a blog post to him, writing, "This new format was advanced by a remarkably effective merger of the immediacy of live theater and the dramatic impact of the cinematic closeup."

Director Van Dirk Fisher and the Riant Theatre placed virtual backdrops behind the actors and the actors, all separated and in some cases in different states, reached out and passed a joint between each other and exited and entered as they stepped in or out of the camera in front of which they performed alone.

The reading took on an immediacy that a staged reading cannot provide, but the degree of difficulty remained almost unnoticed for an audience which tuned in from New York to California.

Judging from the chat rooms and the talk back after the performance, it was a huge success.

The producers were so impressed by what they'd seen they immediately bet the farm and asked him to direct the future Off-Broadway production.

We had only met him in Zoom meetings. He was that impressive.

Last Friday, nearly a year later, finally I received a text from the producer telling me it would finally happen. *The Grace of God & The Man Machine* would open this spring off-Broadway. We were off and running and finally we would be working with Van in person.

Not too long after, I was surprised by a text message from Van's sister:

"Van passed yesterday at 3:49 p.m."

When I called her in disbelief, she told me December of last year, he had been diagnosed with stage four stomach cancer but had fought it and continued to work.

A month or so ago, I contacted him to see if he was interested in working on a new play. He never revealed that he was sick.

Just as American theater is opening up and finally recognizing Black creators, this man and his future audiences will be deprived of his chance to show his considerable gifts.

I would be willing to bet that up until the very end, he believed he was going to beat cancer because that's who he was.

I only knew him through Zoom calls but now he won't even be there for us virtually. I never got a chance to meet him and shake his hand but I know he will be there with us when the play opens.

He will be with us live!

Sometimes You Have to Open the Windows and Listen to the Rain

This morning was hard. I woke up and it was raining. Over the last month, I have been coming to recognize a hard truth — which I finally realized this morning.

Over five years ago, I started this blog to force myself into a weekly discipline and to explore how I could start a whole new career after retirement from a very happy first career as a lawyer.

My whole life I had quietly wanted to see if I could create a life as an artist.

After writing 10 plays for the wonderful little theaters in Baltimore, I decided to see if I could break into New York professional theater, and I took classes at the New York Commercial Theater Institute.

My play *Onaje* was selected by FringeNYC in 2018 and, after great reviews, got picked up and nurtured by a NYC producer. After the rewrites and several table reads to make it a more fleshed out two-act play, *The Grace of God & The Man Machine* was ready.

It was starting to happen, this improbable dream of mine.

But then Covid hit in March of 2020. The theaters shut down just as we were waiting to open off-Broadway.

Then in February of the following year, we were ready again. We planned to open off-Broadway in November, 2022 for a one-month run at Theatre Row on 42nd Street. The dream was coming true!

Then, a month ago, Covid struck again. The producer went out of business after 15 years of producing successful shows.

I looked in the mirror this morning and I said it: "This lifetime dream may not happen."

But then I realized, I'm not ready to give up just yet. Somewhere out there, there may be a theater or a partner or a resource or some other way to make this happen.

I turned away and looked for a diversion, for good news to chase away this awful gathering sadness.

Last week, I learned that my sonnet "Summer Thunderstorms" had been chosen as a runner-up for the Robert Frost Foundation poetry contest this year.

I sat down by the window and reread "Summer Thunderstorm":

Summer Thunderstorms

As with the generations long since dead
The fire and brimstone of the status quo
Wakes him up from the safety of his bed
And lightening frames him in the window

And photographs him in its afterglow.
Tonight he feels his present and its past
As the summer storm also comes and goes.
Conclusions are foolish in a world so vast.

For at the edges of his world and heart
Far past the farthest boundary of his grasp
Where ideas cause worlds to come apart
He lives in this place that will not last.

He loves his life more than he can explain
And leaves the window open to hear the rain.

I opened the windows to hear the rain.

After I looked out at the storm for a little while, I got a fresh cup of coffee and started writing this. I have stuff to do. It's time to get back to work.

A Place to Be

Have You Ever Seen "The Sandlot"?

This is a 4th of July American love story straight from my heart. It doesn't go where you might expect.

In 2013, I sold my controlling interest in the law firm I had created in 1990 and ran for state delegate because I was terrified by the emerging polarization of our country. I lost in a gerrymandered jurisdiction. I never had a chance.

As a child, I hitchhiked through 40 states and met strangers from endlessly different backgrounds and every walk of life.

Back then my rides often came from soldiers who had hitchhiked around the country themselves after the Second World War. They stopped their lives to offer me kindness with no thought of anything in return.

A ranking officer in a top-down convertible drove me into Paris Island, the US Marine training facility, because I could get a carton of Camel cigarettes for 15 cents a pack at the PX. The marching soldiers saluted the license plates as we entered and as he returned me to the road.

I came to understand the unspoken secrets of a country that preached justice and equality but had built its wealth with slave labor on stolen land.

Although we often agreed to disagree, my rides and I shared a national pride. This country had saved a dividing world from fascism and had recently passed legislation like the Civil Rights Act of '64, in an attempt to correct our world at home.

As I traveled shotgun, I learned to listen. That was my job.

We talked and they would tell me about the joy and sadness and insecurity they could not tell their wives. I learned so much from them.

Every ride contained an unspoken understanding that we would never meet again.

The growing polarization that has been dividing us now for years has slowly broken my old hitchhiker's heart.

This 4th of July, my children came home with their loved ones and their children. Last night, we decided to revisit an old movie which they loved to watch each year on the 4th: "The Sandlot."

Because I'm deaf now, I sat in a chair up front facing the TV, my back to them, my face hidden from them as I looked up at the screen.

It is a baseball movie about kids growing up in the late '50s or early '60s. It is nothing but foolishness, but it holds the beauty of a united America that believes in Babe Ruth, the innocence of juvenile behavior, and baseball as a national pastime and religion. James Earl Jones is the linchpin of redemption just because he is, not because it is politically correct.

Sitting with my children and their loved ones and their children behind me, I could cover up ever so gently my unexpected tears as they came.

A Miracle in Rhinestones

Years ago, I met a boy who never once told me the truth but had the heart of a saint.

Back in August 1968, outside of Cheyenne, Wyoming, I was hitchhiking east when a state trooper pulled up next to me. He told me that he was going down the highway for 15 minutes, then turning around, and if I wasn't gone by the time he came back he was going to lock me up in Cheyenne "until I got a court date."

This was serious.

As the officer's taillights disappeared down Interstate 80, I turned around to face the empty road and stuck out my thumb.

I needed a miracle.

As the first car approached, I knelt by the side of the roadway with my hands pressed together simulating prayer.

That car, an old white Ford convertible, was driven by a boy who appeared to be in his mid-20s. He wore a huge cowboy hat, and rhinestones from his shirt collar to his new boots. The boy pulled over and waved for me to get in.

As I thanked him and started to explain my predicament, he laughed and waved off any further conversation. He told me not to worry because he would be driving all night to see his father in Fort Dodge, Iowa.

First car? This guy? It was a miracle... but it gets better.

Next, he asked me if I was hungry. I laughed and nodded yes, and he reached under his seat to hand me a can of peaches, a can opener, and a plastic fork.

He was clearly showing off. You could tell by the grand gestures of his performance and his broad grin. He was having fun.

After I finished the peaches and drained the can of its last sweet syrup, I settled into the ride as he started to talk. He told me that he had been a foreman for the last several years at a ranch, and the night before in Reno, he had girls in the front and back seats of this very car because he had won money in the slots.

As we drove deeper into the night, he told me that before he had been a cowboy he had been a soldier of fortune, and had parachuted into Nicaragua as an agent for the CIA.

His stories were endless and detailed, full of life and love and compassion for those he had worked with, and for the women he had been fortunate to love, as well as those who had broken his heart but had been kind enough to have loved him back for a while.

He was a natural storyteller and the more we relaxed together and talked, the more I liked him for his joy.

Slightly before dawn, when we turned off the Interstate and headed up toward Fort Dodge, he offered a surprising apology: "My old man never amounted to much. He was a postal worker. He drank himself out of the job, but he's always been there for me. He is sick now. I never knew my mom. She left him, but my father, he always has been there for me."

As the light brought color into the outskirts of Fort Dodge, we turned onto a street of freestanding houses in an empty neighborhood with untended lawns, litter on the streets, and an occasional abandoned car.

The door to his father's house was open and the window next to the front door was broken. As we entered, I looked to the right. There was a kitchen with a table and two chairs. To the left was a living room with no furniture. Straight ahead was a staircase with a simple railing and some of the slats missing, which led to a second floor. There were crushed beer cans on the floor and heaping ashtrays on the countertop by the sink.

The boy headed upstairs to go wake up his father. Moments later, there was some heavy coughing from upstairs and muffled voices. There was the sound of crying, raised voices, but also laughter.

After several minutes, an old man slowly navigated the steps and stopped to catch his breath when he reached the bottom step.

The old man apologized for the state of the house and immediately went to the old ice box. He got three beers and proceeded to handed them out. Apparently, these were breakfast beers.

Oddly, the whole house seemed to be filled with love and I felt welcome.

As the sun came up, the two were lost in each other's company, and so I timidly asked if I might be allowed to take a shower since I had been on the road for several days. The old man responded "Sure!" He lit a cigarette and pointed at a wash tub leaning against the kitchen wall. He told me to fill it with hot water from the sink and handed me a big jug of dish washing detergent.

I felt that I could not refuse the kindness. I filled the tub with warm water and detergent, stripped naked, and started to take a bath. The boy and his father paid no attention as they laughed and talked and smoked.

Almost immediately the police arrived, knocked on the unlocked door, then entered. They arrested the boy, put him in handcuffs and shoved him through the door toward the squad car out front. The old man burst into tears. With a beer still in hand, he begged them to release his son as the officers pushed the boy down the walkway and put him in the back seat. The officers never spoke to the pleading old man except to say, "If you touch me, I will take you in, too."

During the entire arrest the police paid no attention to me at all as I sat naked in a wash tub and tried to surround myself with heaps of bubbles.

When the old man returned from the street, he explained through his tears that a week ago his son had finally been released on parole from a Kansas prison. He had been thrown out of school several years before and had been convicted as an adult for smoking marijuana near the school yard. He wasn't a bad kid. Just a free spirit from the wrong side of town.

His father had gotten the old convertible for him and told him he could never outlive his past in Kansas. He told him to go west and "disappear" and never come back again.

The boy had initially agreed, but he had told his father upstairs that he had become homesick for the old man, and he was afraid he would die and the boy would never see his father again.

Everything the boy had told me for the last 12 hours riding through the night was a lie, and also a life he would never have the chance to live.

The old man said he and his son had talked every week during the boy's incarceration and the boy had told him he read all the books and magazines and newspapers he could find in prison.

After the old man had fortified his courage with a few more beers, he marched out the front door and headed toward the police station, which was apparently several miles away.

Alone in the empty house, I dried off with paper towels, slept a little on the living room floor then, in mid-afternoon, hitchhiked to a postal delivery hub. I got a ride from a man driving a mail truck headed east toward Chicago. He told me he'd gotten married the day before and had been up all night. When the driver started to hallucinate dogs running across the Interstate, I volunteered to drive so he could sleep. We switched seats without stopping.

As dawn arrived, with the sleeping driver by my side, I thought about the boy and wondered why he would lie to me all night about a life he never lived, then take me to his home where his lies would surely be revealed.

Maybe it was to show he had a kind heart and a moral code, despite his life. Maybe he just gave up and didn't care. As the sun was coming up in the cab of that mail truck, I realized that I had never asked his name, nor had he asked me mine.

Years later, it occurred to me that no matter how hard I might try, I would never be able find that boy again.

I still think of him often. He was one of the kindest people I have ever met. He has appeared in my poems and plays as a reminder that we really are what we do, not what we say.

A Way of Knowing

As I turned away from Degas' statuette of a dancer at the Musee D'Orsay in Paris last week, I almost missed the imitators. The imitators were lining up, looking at the statuette and striking a pose. The reaction was not mocking and somehow not disrespectful. The imitators were reacting to a man-made object created out of his imagination. The interaction is what mattered.

When I was in high school, I read a line from W. H. Auden that said, "poetry makes nothing happen." It stopped me in my tracks. It was the late '60s. I wanted to do things that made things happen. I became a lawyer. I made things happen.

Now I know I misread the line. Auden was making fun of all those things that appear to make things happen but really don't. Art makes things happen in that it offers the chance to interact with a created object from another person's imagination.

But why does that matter? It seems that at the center of our existence we travel a number of years in the mundane pursuit of what we need to survive, but art offers a conversation with another who is, or has been, on that same journey. It offers, but does not demand, this conversation.

In the same gallery, hordes of people were moving from picture to picture, cell phones out, photographing the exhibit as they hurried by.

They had not accepted the offer. They were just capturing the object.

The imitators had accepted the offer. They were interacting with the Degas' statuette.

The conversation can happen in many forums, but it is always between the artist and the self. It can come through some or all the senses. It can be theoretical. It can come with an artist's demand for your attention, as with Andy Warhol asking you to notice common objects, but for me it is always a very personal person-to-person communication.

It can also be environmental. On my way home, I noticed the statues in the park and the park in the city as I walk through. The art of the statue inside the art of the park surrounded by the mundane existence of the traffic and commerce of the city.

I found Auden's quote:

"For poetry makes nothing happen: it survives
In the valley of its making where executives
Would never want to tamper, flows on south
From ranches of isolation and the busy griefs,
Raw towns that we believe and die in; it survives,
A way of happening, a mouth."

In Memory of W.B.Yeats (d. Jan. 1939)

He says all this better than I but I had to learn it for myself.

The Older You Get the Shorter Your Stories Should Be

Out of the Rain and into Ice House Pond

Out of the rain of last week...

I'm back to work. Watch me pitch.

As a child growing up in New England I quickly adopted "Yankee ingenuity" and I completely embraced "self-reliance," which required me to not work for others during summer vacation in case I felt an urgent need to go to the beach.

One summer back in the late 1960s, two high school friends and I started the "Right On House Painting Company." This was a highly independent entrepreneurial effort.

Our advertising amounted to a forceful announcement of the company name followed by the lifting of our right fist to the sky and pledging solemnly: "Right On"!

We were, of course, saluting latex paint.

Because we were under-funded and had to keep the overhead low, we lived in an old barn off of Upper Lambert's Cove Road, which we rented from a local commercial fisherman who had at least twenty cats and had been drunk all winter.

We struck a deal for $15 a week rent if we would help him remove the long johns he had been wearing all winter.

Despite the bargain rent, he got the better deal.

We cleaned out the barn and divided it into quadrants so each of us had a room and there was a room left for eating, drinking and entertaining.

It was our "green" corporate headquarters.

We had no running water but refused to live without elegance, so we built an outhouse in a birch grove with a white wicker chair with the bottom cut out of it. We were proud to be feeding the birch trees.

We were way ahead of our time.

We bathed nearby in Ice House Pond — pretty much always at night so we didn't get our bathing suits wet.

To reduce automotive and travel expenses, we generally hitchhiked with a can of paint and a brush in one hand and our thumb extended from the other in order to get to work.

It was also an early form of targeted corporate advertising, since we ended up meeting everybody on Martha's Vineyard over the summer.

Every ride was a job interview from the passenger's seat, but it didn't matter because we were on your way to work anyway.

Our corporate mission statement required that on sunny days we went to the beach. On rainy days, we played poker. On hazy days we painted houses.

We made good money.

When asked about our profit margins we would announce: "Enough is as good as a feast" and drop our eyes and lift our fist to the sky.

My entrepreneurial spirit has never died.

I have avoided being an employee over the last several decades by starting a law firm and retiring to become a poet and here I am selling my book, *An Accidental Diary*... but man do I have a deal for you!

It's all about how you look at things.

Don't look at this book as poetry — everybody hates poetry and a book of sonnets is worse.

But! If you look at it like sort of a Bible written in rhyme and rhythm or maybe just "Easy Go'n Bob's Book of Random Wisdom," then why not?

Keep it where you can read just one sonnet at a time uninterrupted. Like the bathroom. Or a wicker chair with a hole in it. I'm not proud.

Consider the sonnet entitled "The Facts of Life," obviously composed for future generations.

The Facts of Life

I swam, back then, with some father's daughters,
Back stroking only slightly out of touch,
Out to the raft in the starry waters
And never thought of their fathers all that much.

My child, don't judge me till you're fifty-five
But there were midnight visits to "Ice House Pond,"
In my misspent youth, when I was still alive,
Where couples would strip, and swim and then bond.

And my child, this I know for sure is true:
At seventeen we all are born to be free
But 'cause I'm your father and I love you
Please consider this seasoned advice from me:

As you lust for life, avoid the crudity
But don't miss occasional sponti-nudity.

Right On!

(I hope you'll get a copy and, after you have read it, give it away: *https://robertbowiejr.com/booklink.*)

Acknowledgements

These stories cover decades of friends, family, colleagues, and acquaintances, plus adventures on multiple continents. So, of course, there are far too many people to thank properly.

However, I would be remiss if I didn't mention a few, with apologies to everyone I've inadvertently omitted.

First and foremost, to Susan Chase, my muse — and our families past and present — I thank you each from the bottom of my heart.

Jeanette Yocum, my friend and assistant for over 30 years, without whom this book would not have been possible.

Stephanie Fowler and the team at Salt Water Media. My advisors on the book, including editor and designer Parker Bennett, publicist Katie Marinello, and my lawyer, Kaitlin Corey, Esq.

The generous people who read this book and offered kind words and blurbs including Drew Faust, Ben Bradlee, Jr., Ty Cobb, Stephen Eich, Belinda Rathbone, Katya Chelli, Mel Edden, Dan Cuddy, Virginia Giritlian, Sherry Rudick, Cathy Welty, Bolling Willse, Carin Coyle and *The Loch Raven Review*.

The many friends and followers whose support on social media increased my confidence and gave this book its life. Too many to mention, but I'll mention just a few: Woody Bennett, Trearty Bingle, Steven Bloomfield, Alan Bussard, Brian Butler, Ellen Butler, T.B. Carrigan, Priscilla Carroll, Richard Chisolm, Judy Dobbs & Bob Condlin, Susan Donahue & Chuck Cross, Kyle & Tom Cummins, Buzz Cusack, George Deptula, Anna Dibble, M.J. & Tom Dickson, Judith Dollenmayer, Liz & Dan Fesperman, Kate Freed, Maria & Daniel Gerrity, Mark Gately,

Kate Gellert, Jack Gohn, Faith & John Hawks, Christina Hilton, Cindy & Ron Holland, Ed Houff, Lura Johnson, Robert Krim, Joey Kroart, Katie Lapp, Shawn Moran, Philip Lovejoy & Jim Moses, Marilyn & Lee Ogburn, Ken Ledeen, Larry Nathans, Kathy & Michael Oles, Alan Orth, Wendy Shattuck & Sam Plimpton and family, Louisa Putnan, Liza Rathbone, Peter Rathbone, David Robinette, Joanne & Neil Ruther, Shawn Sturgeon, Tom Swift, Pote Videt, Edwin Warfield, Cathy Welty, Bibi & Fred Walton, Jen & Henry Wyner.

Rachel Lamson and Philip Lovejoy from the Harvard Alumni Association, Jane & Jack Reardon, Marion Dry and ClassAct'73, and the helpful photo archivists at Harvard University and Vassar College.

My mentors and friends who helped support my playwrighting efforts: Laura Lundy, Sue Conover Marinello and all the Marinello family, Christian Dé Grey Cárdenas, Tom Viertel of the O'Neill National Playwrights Conference and the New York State Theatre Institute. And, of course, Richard Jackson, and the many excellent little theaters of Baltimore.

Candace Currie, who helped inspire my first collection of sonnets. Helena Minton and the Robert Frost Foundation. Angelo Otterbein and the wonderful Manor Mill, Mel Edden, who brought new voices in poetry into my life, including poets and readers Shirley J. Brewer, Matt Hohner, Jennifer Keith, Alan Reese and Mike Fallon (who teaches at Hereford Library in conjunction with Manor Mill's Poetry Open Mic).

Emma Snyder and Hannah Fenster and their team at The Ivy Bookshop in Baltimore, The Grolier Poetry Book Shop in Cambridge, and all of the amazing independent book sellers everywhere.

About the Author

Robert Bowie, Jr. has worked as a house painter, bartender, lawyer, adjunct professor, poet, author, and playwright. He lives in Maryland.

He has had 10 plays produced, including *Onaje*, which premiered with five sold-out performances at FringeNYC in 2018. An expanded version is currently in development.

Bob's well-reviewed collection of sonnets, *An Accidental Diary*, is available to order online: *https://robertbowiejr.com/booklink*.

Bob continues to post regularly on his blog at *https://robertbowiejr.com*.

RobertBowieJr.com
facebook.com/robertbowiejrplaywright
twitter.com/robertbowiejr
instagram.com/robertbowiejr

www.ingramcontent.com/pod-product-compliance
Lightning Source LLC
Chambersburg PA
CBHW050854160426
43194CB00011B/2148